2 Corinthians

A Digest of Reformed Comment

2 Corinthians

A Digest of Reformed Comment

GEOFFREY B. WILSON

MINISTER OF BIRKBY BAPTIST CHURCH
HUDDERSFIELD

THE BANNER OF TRUTH TRUST

THE BANNER OF TRUTH TRUST
3 Murrayfield Road, Edinburgh EH 12 6EL
78b Chiltern Street, London WIM IPS
P.O. Box 652, Carlisle, Pa 17013, U.S.A.

*

© Geoffrey B. Wilson 1973
First published 1973
ISBN 0 85151 168 6

*

Set in 11 on 12 pt Bembo
and printed in Great Britain by
Hunt Barnard Printing Ltd,
Aylesbury, Bucks.

CONTENTS

ACKNOWLEDGEMENTS

I am grateful to all the authors and publishers who have permitted me to quote from their works, and in particular to the Rev. Professor P. E. Hughes of Westminster Theological Seminary, whose commentary in the New London series is compulsory reading for all serious students of the Epistle. I would like to add a word of special thanks to Mr S. M. Houghton M. A. and to the Rev. W. J. Cook B. A., B.D. for the benefit of their judicious advice on many difficult points. I am also indebted to Dr. Williams' Library and to the Evangelical Library for their generous assistance. While I am glad to acknowledge the helpfulness of modern versions (RSV, NEB, and Moffatt) at certain points, their use should not be taken as a blanket endorsement of the theological liberalism they so often reflect.

Huddersfield   GEOFFREY WILSON
July 1972

ACKNOWLEDGEMENTS

INTRODUCTION

After staying over eighteen months Paul left the flourishing church he had founded in Corinth for Ephesus, where it seems he received disquieting news of the lax conduct of his Corinthian converts. [Acts 18] It was to deal with this grave situation that he resolved to pay them a second visit which evidently proved to be a painful experience, for the Corinthians did not prove amenable to apostolic discipline. [2:1; 12:21] This unhappy encounter was followed by a letter since lost in which he warned them of the serious consequences of such licentious behaviour. [1 Cor 5:9]

Shortly after the despatch of that letter, more bad news reached Paul from Corinth [1 Cor 1:11;12; 5:1], but this was mercifully offset by the arrival of the Corinthian deputies, Stephanas, Fortunatus, and Achaicus. [1 Cor 16:17] For though the letter they presumably brought with them made no mention of the grievous disorders of which he had been independently informed, the very fact that the church still sought his advice on certain points of conduct and discipline showed that it had not entirely renounced his authority. The stern reproofs Paul had to administer in his reply (the canonical 'First' Corinthians) cost him 'much affliction and anguish of heart' [2:4], yet it was a price which he did not hesitate to pay for he knew that there could be no amendment without repentance. [7:9;10] Since it was undesirable for Paul to arrive in Corinth until he was assured that his 'severe' letter had done its work well, he postponed his projected visit [1 Cor 16:5-7], and anxiously awaited the news of its reception from Titus with whom he had sent it.

After the riot in Ephesus brought his work there to an abrupt end [Acts 20:1], Paul hastened to Troas where he had arranged to meet Titus on his return from Corinth. [2:12;13] The disappointment of this hope led him to travel on to Macedonia, where at last they met, probably in Philippi or its port, Neapolis. The report that Titus gave to Paul on the situation in Corinth was largely reassuring. Although the false teachers, who had infiltrated into the church by arming themselves with letters of recommendation [3:1], were encouraging a minority to remain recalcitrant [12:21], the majority were humbled by the apostle's letter and had indeed 'sorrowed to repentance.' [2:12;13; 7:5ff.] Under the inspiration of the Spirit, Paul here gives free expression to the mingled emotions which were aroused in him by this report. It is this deliberate lack of reserve that makes the document we know as Second Corinthians the most intensely personal of all Paul's utterances. It is at once a triumphant vindication of his apostolic ministry, and a searing indictment of the pretensions of the 'super-apostles' who were attempting to overthrow his work in Corinth by basely slandering his character and his motives. Thus the purpose of the letter was to prepare the Corinthians for his promised visit. It was written to ensure that when he came to Corinth for the *third* time it would be in joy and not in sorrow or anger. [2:1; 12:14; 13:1;2]

As Second Corinthians is manifestly an intelligible unity, there would seem to be no good reason for accepting the modern notion that it contains fragments of other letters that Paul is supposed to have written to the Corinthians, especially as there is no external evidence to show that it was ever circulated in any other form.

CHAPTER ONE

V1: **Paul, an apostle of Jesus Christ by the will of God, and Timothy our brother, unto the church of God which is at Corinth, with all the saints which are in all Achaia:**

Paul, an apostle of Christ Jesus through the will of God, (RV) Since the Corinthians had questioned his authority so recently, it is not surprising that Paul should begin with the reminder that he is not an apostle of Christ Jesus by human accreditation but by divine appointment. It is through the eternal good pleasure of God that he is such an apostle. Moreover, because he was *directly* called by the risen Christ Himself, his apostleship differed radically from that which was exercised by those who were *mediately* commissioned by the church [8:23; *Phil* 2:25]. And though he counts it a privilege to serve the church [4:5], it is significant that he never speaks of himself as 'an apostle of the church.' All the evidence 'points overwhelmingly to the fact that, *in the highest sense of the word*, only the original apostles and Paul were called and appointed to be the "authorized representatives" of the exalted Lord. Where Barnabas is called an apostle in Acts 14:4, 14 it is clearly in the sense of one being sent by the Church as a fully commissioned missionary but not as an "apostle of Christ" [cf. *Acts* 13:14] in the highest sense as used of the Twelve and Paul.' (Norval Geldenhuys, *Supreme Authority*, pp 71–72)

[13]

Thus as it was the unique function of the apostles to be *eye*-witnesses of the resurrection and by their inspired testimony to provide the foundation upon which the Church rests, it is evident that they can have no successors in this office.

and Timothy the brother, (RV margin) It is not to share the responsibility of composition that Paul includes Timothy in the address, but to enhance his appeal to the Corinthians. What he writes with all the authority of an apostle also commands the fraternal assent of a fellow-Christian who is well known to them. [1 *Cor* 1:1]

unto the church of God which is at Corinth, In writing to this company of believers living in a particular place, Paul reminds them of the dignity that is theirs as *the* Church of God, and of their obligations as members of the Church *of God*. According to K. L. Schmidt, the designation affords strong support for 'the contention that the Church is not a great community made up of an accumulation of small communities, but is truly present in its wholeness in every company of believers, however small.' (quoted by P. E. Hughes)

with all the saints which are in the whole of Achaia: (RV) Paul addresses the Corinthian church *directly*, and all the Christians in the province *indirectly*. This indicates that he 'was conscious that his written words were significant for the whole Church of God, and not merely for the particular local churches at which they were first delivered.' (Tasker) In the New Testament sainthood is not the prerogative of a special caste but the privilege of every Christian. [cf. *Acts* 9:13] As each believer is objectively 'holy' in Christ, so he is to be subjectively transformed 'into the same image.' [3:18] This does not mean, however, 'that these "saints" never sin after becoming saints [*Phil* 3:12, Paul; 1 *John* 1:8–10; John].' (Lenski)

[14]

V2: **Grace be to you and peace from God our Father, and from the Lord Jesus Christ.**

Grace to you and peace (RV) It is by replacing the ordinary 'hail' of Greek letter-writing with the word 'grace' that Paul invests the customary greeting with a deep religious meaning. (Menzies) ' "Grace" is the free favour of God; "peace" is the condition which results from its reception.' (Goudge)

from God our Father and the Lord Jesus Christ. The pronoun 'our' advertises the stupendous fact that God the Father is also the Father of believers in virtue of His adoptive grace towards them in the Lord Jesus Christ. (John Murray) The blessings of grace and peace descend to us from God our Father 'as the primal *Fountain*,' through Christ 'as the mediatorial *Channel*'; 'and by coupling both Persons in one and the same invocation, their equality in the Godhead is brightly confirmed.' (Brown)

V3: **Blessed be God, even the Father of our Lord Jesus Christ, the Father of mercies, and the God of all comfort;**

Blessed be the God and Father of our Lord Jesus Christ, (RV) Paul usually follows his greeting with a thanksgiving for what God has done for his readers, but here he bursts into a jubilant doxology to praise God for the marvellous mercies so recently vouchsafed to himself. (*v* 4) This remarkable expression indicates that God is both the God and Father of the Lord Jesus Christ; He became His God when the Son was made flesh for our salvation, whereas He is His Father from all eternity. [cf. 1 Pet 1:3] But we cannot call upon God as *our* Father (*v* 2) except as we are related to Him through the merits and mediation of *our* Lord Jesus Christ. [*John* 14:6]

the Father of the compassions (Lenski) 'Instead of speaking, as we should, of "the compassion of God" as an abstract principle, Paul speaks of its various concrete manifestations. These reveal the essential nature of the great Father and are therefore taken up into His Name.' (Beet) [*Ps* 103:13]

and God of all comfort; (RV) This word which Paul uses ten times in five verses is not to be understood in any sentimental sense. God comforts His people by encouraging and strengthening them, so that they are not crushed by affliction. Pink points out that this is an excellency peculiar to the true and living God, for the heathen deities are represented as being so cruel and ferocious that even their own worshippers regard them as objects of dread. Yet 'many believers seem to be as reluctant to go out of themselves to God alone for comfort, as unbelievers are to go out of themselves to Christ alone for righteousness.'

*V*4: **Who comforteth us in all our tribulation, that we may be able to comfort them which are in any trouble, by the comfort wherewith we ourselves are comforted of God.**

tribulation . . . trouble = affliction (RV) This is the distress that is produced by painful pressure, which is relieved by the comfort that prevents it from becoming insupportable. Knowing the sustaining strength of God in *all* his affliction qualified the apostle to be of comfort to others in *every kind* of affliction. He did not see this comfort as a blessing to be selfishly kept to himself, but as the divinely given means of helping those in similar straits. Paul would have the Corinthians know that he finds such comforting more congenial than administering the faithful wounds of a friend. [*Prov* 27:6] For though he had not flinched from this duty, he did not rejoice in it.

*V*5: **For as the sufferings of Christ abound in us, so our consolation also aboundeth by Christ.**

For as Christ's sufferings flow over abundantly to us, even so our comfort also aboundeth through Christ. (Bernard) It is not suggested that the glorified Christ continues to suffer with Paul in these afflictions; the thought is rather that those who are identified with Christ by faith cannot avoid their share of the very same hatred that reached its dreadful climax in His crucifixion. It is therefore only as Christ's reproach is willingly borne that this suffering is swallowed up by Christ's comfort. [*Rom* 8:17; *Phil* 3:10; *Col* 1:24; *Heb* 13:13] 'As union with Christ was the source of the afflictions which Paul endured, so it was the source of the abundant consolation which he enjoyed. This makes the great difference between the sorrows of believers and those of unbelievers. Alienation from Christ does not secure freedom from suffering, but it cuts us off from the only source of consolation. Therefore the sorrow of the world worketh death.' (Hodge)

*V*6: **And whether we be afflicted, it is for your consolation and salvation, which is effectual in the enduring of the same sufferings which we also suffer: or whether we be comforted, it is for your consolation and salvation.**

But whether we are afflicted, it is for your comfort and salvation; or whether we are comforted, it is for your comfort, which worketh in the patient enduring of the same sufferings which we also suffer. (ARV) So vital is the bond that unites Paul with the Corinthians that whatever befalls him in the service of Christ is experienced with a view to their good. He endures affliction for their encouragement and salvation; he receives comfort for their strengthening, the effectiveness of which is shown in their patient endurance of the same suffering for the sake of the gospel as he himself endures.

*V*7: **And our hope of you is stedfast, knowing, that as ye are partakers of the sufferings, so shall ye be also of the consolation.**

And our hope for you is stedfast; knowing that, as ye are partakers of the sufferings, so also are ye of the comfort. (RV) Paul sums up the paragraph on a note of triumphant hope. It is because the Corinthians are sharers with him both in his sufferings and in his comfort that he has no doubt of their final salvation. They will be enabled to endure to the end for the comfort is always commensurate with the suffering. That Paul could speak in this way of his recent relations with them affords astonishing proof of his largeness of heart. 'He does not claim the credit of comforting them: they receive comfort from the same source that he does – from God through Christ.' (Plummer)

*V*8: **For we would not, brethren, have you ignorant of our trouble which came to us in Asia, that we were pressed out of measure, above strength, insomuch that we despaired even of life:**

For we would not have you ignorant, brethren, concerning our affliction which befell us in Asia, that we were weighed down exceedingly, beyond our power, insomuch that we despaired even of life: (RV) Having spoken in a general way of affliction and comfort, Paul now vividly recalls a recent affliction by which he was so excessively weighed down that he even despaired of life. Clearly he had been in mortal peril of some kind, though in the absence of further information it is impossible to identify the nature of this experience. However, Paul's concern was not to provide a circumstantial account of the danger, but to magnify God's grace in his deliverance from it. (*v* 9)

*V*9: **But we had the sentence of death in ourselves, that we should not trust in ourselves, but in God which raiseth the dead:**

Yea, we ourselves have had the sentence of death within ourselves, (RV margin) Denney draws attention to the force of the perfect tense: 'We *had* this experience, and in its fruit – a newer and deeper faith in God – we *have* it still. It is a permanent possession in this happy form.' If Paul now recalls the sentence he had passed on himself in his despair it is only that the Corinthians might learn the blessed lesson he was taught by it. For no trial however severe can frustrate the sovereign purpose of Him who does in fact work all things together for the good of His people. [*Rom* 8:28]

that we should not trust in ourselves, but in God which raiseth the dead: Thus the affliction that dealt the fatal stroke to all self-trust was sent to inspire undying hope in the God by whose omnipotent power alone the dead are raised to life. It is this capacity to create life where previously death reigned supreme that distinguishes the one true and living God from all the helpless deities of man's invention. [*Ps* 135: 15-18; *Ezek* 37:1-14 *Rom* 4:17; *Heb* 11:19]

*V*10: **Who delivered us from so great a death, and doth deliver: in whom we trust that he will yet deliver us;**

Who delivered us out of so great a death, and will deliver: on whom we have set our hope that he will also still deliver us; (RV) Having experienced so great a deliverance, Paul cannot doubt that the God upon whom he has set his hope will continue to deliver him from whatever perils still lie ahead until he is finally delivered from suffering and brought to glory. [2 *Tim* 4:18]

*V*11: **Ye also helping together by prayer for us, that for the gift bestowed upon us by the means of many persons thanks may be given by many on our behalf.**

Paul here gently reminds the Corinthians that they are not idle spectators of a drama in which they have no part to play. For it is by their joining together in prayer on his behalf that he expects to obtain this deliverance which remains the gracious gift of God, even though its bestowal involves the supplication of many. Yet the great end for which such answers to prayer are given is never secured by the mere reception of the blessing itself, but in that grateful response which magnifies the glory of the Blesser Himself. Hence the undeserved favours that descend to us from God must ever ascend to God as a heartfelt paean of praise. [cf. 4:15; 9:11]

*V*12: **For our rejoicing is this, the testimony of our conscience, that in simplicity and godly sincerity, not with fleshly wisdom, but by the grace of God, we have had our conversation in the world, and more abundantly to you-ward.**

Paul can enlist the support of the Corinthians in prayer with confidence, for he is satisfied that his conduct in the world and the life he lived among them for no less than eighteen months are a sufficient reply to the vile calumnies of those who assailed his integrity and impugned his sincerity in order to establish themselves as the new leaders of the church. [cf. *Heb* 13:18]

For our glorying is this, (RV) Since Paul is not ashamed of what the grace of God has wrought in his life, he does not hesitate to counter the empty boasting of his opponents in Corinth with a true glorying in the Lord (contrast 11:18 with 10:17).

the testimony of our conscience, This testimony is true, for he knows the real peace of a conscience pacified by the blood of Christ, and the sure guidance of a conscience enlightened by the Word of God.

that in holiness and sincerity of God, not in fleshly wisdom but in the grace of God, we behaved ourselves in the world, (RV) Thus Paul freely attributes the 'moral purity' (Arndt-Gingrich) of his conduct and the sincerity of his motives to the grace of God. He has moved in the sphere of this grace ever since the day he renounced all confidence in the flesh, including that fleshly wisdom upon which the Corinthians set such store, and which he had tried so hard to discourage in them. [1 Cor 2:1ff]

and more abundantly to you-ward. He was of course equally sincere elsewhere but the Corinthians had been given a better opportunity than most to observe his sincerity. 'He has deliberately put it this way to show that there was no need for witnesses from a distance, for they themselves were the best witnesses to all that he had said.' (Calvin)

*V*13: **For we write none other things unto you, than what ye read or acknowledge; and I trust ye shall acknowledge even to the end;**

*V*14: **As also ye have acknowledged us in part, that we are your rejoicing, even as ye also are ours in the day of the Lord Jesus.**

For we write you nothing but what you can read and

[21]

understand; (RSV) Moreover, Paul insists that he is as sincere in his letters as he is in his life. He is not the shifty correspondent his detractors claim him to be, writing one thing and meaning another. He always writes what he means, and means exactly what he writes. 'You don't have to read between the lines of my letters; you can understand them.' (Moffatt) But their reception of his 'previous' letter [1 Cor 5:9] had shown that they were not always willing to understand the plain meaning of what he had written. The obscurity of Scripture lies not in the supposed difficulty of its message, but in that spiritual insensitivity which cherishes the sins Scripture so clearly condemns.

I hope you will understand fully, as you have understood in part, that you can be proud of us as we can be of you, on the day of the Lord Jesus. (RSV) Paul here contrasts 'the imperfect estimate of his sincerity which the Corinthians now have with that which will be theirs when the secrets of all hearts are revealed at the Last Day.' (Chrysostom cited by Plummer) When they at last realize all that they owe to his ministry, they will be as proud of him as he is of them. [1 Thess 2:19, 20]

V15: And in this confidence I was minded to come unto you before, that ye might have a second benefit;

V16: And to pass by you into Macedonia, and to come again out of Macedonia unto you, and of you to be brought on my way toward Judaea.

It was on the ground of this mutual confidence that Paul had expressed the hope of paying the Corinthians a double visit, on his way to and from Macedonia, so that they might receive a 'second benefit' and be given the privilege of sending him forward on his journey to Judaea. Probably Paul had informed them of his original intention in the 'previous' letter, but he was led to abandon it by the grave news that called forth the 'severe' letter in which he also acquainted them with this change in his plans. [1 *Cor* 16:5–7]

*V*17: **When I therefore was thus minded, did I use lightness? or the things that I purpose, do I purpose according to the flesh, that with me there should be yea yea, and nay nay?**

Was such a change of plan evidence of the 'fickleness' (RV) of character attributed to Paul by his opponents in Corinth? Or can the Corinthians believe that their Apostle makes his plans in such an unprincipled manner that he has no compunction in affirming one thing at one time and shortly changing to the very opposite? The unjust allegations of his critics are not merely echoed but emphatically answered in these indignant questions.

*V*18: **But as God is true, our word toward you was not yea and nay.**

But as God is faithful, our word toward you is not yea and nay. (RV) The Corinthians should realize that they could not call in question the trustworthiness of their apostle without also reflecting upon the faithfulness of God who had entrusted him with the gospel. For was it not the height of incongruity to imagine that a faithful God had saved them through the ministrations of a faithless servant? Experience should have taught them above all others that he is not a man of Jesuitical reserve who means 'No' when he says 'Yes.' Thus 'God is faithful in the fact that he sends men to preach whose preaching is not double-tongued, a promise and no performance.' (Massie)

[23]

*V*19: **For the Son of God, Jesus Christ, who was preached among you by us, even by me and Silvanus and Timotheus, was not yea and nay, but in him was yea.**

For the Son of God, Jesus Christ, 'Proof of the unchangeableness of the doctrine from the unchangeableness of the subject of it – viz., Jesus Christ. He is called "the Son of God," to show the impossibility of change in One co-equal with God Himself [cf. 1 *Sam* 15:29; *Mal* 3:6].' (Fausset).

who was preached among you by us, even by me and Silvanus and Timothy, was not yea and nay, (RV) 'The point is that the Corinthians had trusted these instruments of God, had trusted their message and their character, for the two went together. No mighty yea-Christ could have been transmitted by yea-and-nay heralds.' (Lenski) [*Acts* 18:5]

but in him is yea. (RV) The force of this is well conveyed by P. E. Hughes: 'In Him yes was and continues to be a reality.' The Corinthians dare not suspect the fidelity of their teachers unless they are prepared to doubt the validity of their faith. For the divine reality proclaimed by these faithful messengers had been marvellously verified in their own experience. It is Christ Himself who proves the truth of the gospel through the witness of the Spirit in the hearts of His people. [*v* 22; *Gal* 3:2]

*V*20: **For all the promises of God in him are yea, and in him Amen, unto the glory of God by us.**

For how many soever be the promises of God, in him is the yea: (RV) Christ is the fulfiller and fulfilment of all the promises of God because He is the sum and substance of them. From Genesis to Malachi – from the *protevangelium*, the first promise of a Redeemer, to prophecy's last witness to His coming – each and every promise finds its affirmation and accomplishment in Him. [*Luke* 24:44; *Gal* 3:16; *Heb* 10:7]

wherefore also through him is the Amen, unto the glory of God (RV) Christ's 'Yea' to all the Divine promises is appropriated by the 'Amen' of faith. In affixing this seal to His faithfulness, faith gives glory to God. [*John* 3:33; *Rom* 4:20] It is both through Christ and through those who preach Him ('through us') that men are brought to say the 'Amen' of faith. For though Christ is the great awakener of faith, 'His appeal reaches the world through His representatives.' (Goudge) [*Rom* 10:17]

through us. (RV) 'This connects the thought with the main argument. Is it likely that we should be unfaithful to promises who cause glory to be ascribed to God for His faithfulness?' (Massie)

V21: **Now he which establisheth us with you in Christ, and hath anointed us, is God;**

V22: **Who hath also sealed us, and given the earnest of the Spirit in our hearts.**

Now he that establisheth us with you into Christ, (RV margin) As the Corinthians were divinely constrained to *confirm* Paul's preaching of the gospel with the 'Amen' of faith, so it is no less a work of grace that they with him are being daily *confirmed* in their union with Christ. Nor could they consider the reality of this shared experience without recognizing that he is sincere and consistent in all his relations with them. Moreover, Paul goes on to show that God's *present* work of establishing all believers in Christ is based entirely upon what He has *already* done for them in conversion. For it was then that He anointed, sealed, and gave the earnest of the Spirit to them.

and anointed us, is God; (RV) It is in the anointing of His people by the Holy Spirit that God consecrates them to His service and makes them like Christ, the Anointed One *par excellence*. [*Luke* 4:18, 19; 1 *John* 2:20, 27] Hence this blessing is bestowed through Christ, 'on whom the oil of gladness, and all the graces of the Spirit are first poured out, and then from Him are carried to the meanest member of His body.' (David Dickson on Psalm 133) [cf. *John* 7:39]

who also sealed us, (RV) The sealing of the Spirit is the act by which God marks out a people for Himself and secures them unto the day of redemption. The Holy Spirit 'marks those in whom he dwells as belonging to God. They bear the seal of God upon them. *Rev* 7:2, 2 *Tim* 2:19 . . . He also bears witness in the hearts of believers that they are the children of God. He authenticates them to themselves and others as genuine believers. And he effectually secures them from apostasy and perdition. *Eph* 1:13, 4:30.' (Hodge)

and gave us the earnest of the Spirit in our hearts. (RV) The 'deposit' or 'pledge' of the Spirit is at once the foretaste and guarantee of the Christian's interest in the heavenly inheritance. [*Rom* 8:23; 2 *Cor* 5:5; *Eph* 1:14] And though the life he now lives is of the same kind as that which he will enjoy hereafter 'the present gift of the Spirit is only a *small fraction* of the future endowment. This idea also would be suggested by the usual relation between the earnest-money and the full payment.' (Lightfoot)

*V*23: **Moreover I call God for a record upon my soul, that to spare you I came not as yet unto Corinth.**
Having demonstrated the impossibility of any duplicity on his part, the apostle now reveals the real reason for delaying his visit to them. Since no one else knew what caused him to change his mind, he solemnly appeals to God to confirm the truthfulness of his testimony ('for a witness upon my soul'

RV). In fact it was solely to spare them that he came 'not any more' to Corinth. It was out of the question to gloss over the grievous news of their immorality and indiscipline, but he thought it better to write a painful letter rather than pay them another painful visit. [2:4] For had he been present in person he must have proceeded against them with even greater severity.

*V*24: **Not for that we have dominion over your faith, but are helpers of your joy: for by faith ye stand.**

To prevent his detractors from misinterpreting this explanation, Paul assures the Corinthians that he has no desire to exercise any 'lordship' (RV) over their faith, but seeks only to remove those sinful disorders which hinder their true rejoicing. Thus if even the apostles did not regard it as one of their functions to play at 'being lords over God's heritage' then how can such power lawfully be claimed and exercised by their pretended successors? [cf. 1 *Pet* 5:1-3]

for in faith ye stand fast. (ARV) 'Well may we disclaim any such undue interference; for ye stand, not on us, but each to his own Master on the footing of his own faith; nor can any one, not even an apostle of Jesus Christ, come in between him and God, the Judge of all.' (Brown) [*Rom* 14:4]

CHAPTER TWO

*V*1: **But I determined this with myself, that I would not come again to you in heaviness.**

As the argument is continued, the unfortunate chapter division should be ignored. Paul not only wanted to spare the Corinthians, he also wished to spare himself the grief of a second painful visit. [12:14; 13:1f] Accordingly he had reached this resolve, 'not to come to you again in sorrow.' (Arndt-Gingrich) Nevertheless he had deferred his visit in their interest, and not simply to avoid further personal suffering. His decision was made in the hope that this delay would give them the opportunity to put matters right themselves, following their reception of his 'severe' letter (i.e. 1 Corinthians).

*V*2: **For if I make you sorry, who is he then that maketh me glad, but the same which is made sorry by me?**

If I pain you, then who is to give me pleasure? None but the very people I am paining! (Moffatt) Paul had postponed his visit because it was no pleasure for him to give pain to the only people who could bring him joy. Their follies had forced him to grieve them, but that also grieved him. Hence the restoration of his joy depended upon their repentance and amendment.

*V*3: **And I wrote this same unto you, lest, when I came, I should have sorrow from them of whom I ought to rejoice; having confidence in you all, that my joy is the joy of you all.**

And I wrote this very thing, (RV) It was for this reason that he wrote to tell them of his change of plan, a change that was prompted by his love for them! [1 *Cor* 16:5-8]

lest, when I came, I should have sorrow from them of whom I ought to rejoice; For if the apostle came to a dis-affected and rebellious people, then his grief would prevent him from fulfilling the proper end of his ministry, which was the promotion of their joy. [1:24]

having confidence in you all, that my joy is the joy of you all. 'Even at this time of revolt he had confidence that they had no real joy apart from his, and would therefore put away what was grievous to him.' (Massie) [cf. the 'all' of 13:14]

*V*4: **For out of much affliction and anguish of heart I wrote unto you with many tears; not that ye should be grieved, but that ye might know the love which I have more abundantly unto you.**

This is a touching disclosure of what it cost the apostle to write his 'severe' letter. 'We take this letter to which Paul refers to be First Corinthians. The critics disagree. They fail to find the tears about which Paul speaks. They catalogue the pas-sages where Paul may have and where he could not have shed tears when he was dictating First Corinthians. The view that the whole letter must be dripping with tears, that all of the emotion of the writer must lie revealed on the surface, in fact, that his tears ought to be mentioned in the proper places where he had shed them is unwarranted.' (Lenski)

[29]

Indeed it is impossible to imagine such a man as Paul remaining impassive in the face of the scandalous disorders which are mirrored in 1 Corinthians.

not that ye should be made sorry, but that ye might know the love which I have more abundantly unto you. (RV) It gave Paul no satisfaction to make them sorry, but he loved them too much to let them lie down in their sins. 'By writing, rather than immediately coming to them in person with a rod, he lovingly afforded them an opportunity for self-examination, repentance, and reformation.' (P. E. Hughes) [1 Cor 4:21] 'More abundantly' should not of course be taken to mean that Paul loved the Corinthians more than his converts in other places.

V5: **But if any have caused grief, he hath not grieved me, but in part: that I may not overcharge you all.**

But if any hath caused sorrow, he hath caused sorrow, not to me, (RV) Paul here delicately alludes to the immoral man whom he had directed the Corinthians to excommunicate. [1 Cor 5:1-5] He wants them to understand that his insistence on their passing this sentence upon the offender was not due to any sense of personal grievance on his part. For while he could not but grieve over the man's sin, he was not the party who had been injured by it.

but in some degree (in order not to say too much) to you all. (Arndt-Gingrich) Although Paul has no wish to exaggerate the consequences of the offence, the least he can say is that the injury inflicted extended to the whole congregation of which this man was a member. For all who tolerated the sin were damaged by it. [1 Cor 5:2] (Beet)

V6: **Sufficient to such a man is this punishment, which was inflicted of many.**

As the penalty imposed by the majority obedient to the apostle had led the offender to repent of his sin, he should now be restored to the communion of the church. For the aim of all such discipline 'is, in the last resort, the restoration of the fallen.' (Denney) [1 Cor 5:5]

V7: **So that contrariwise ye ought rather to forgive him, and comfort him, lest perhaps such a one should be swallowed up with overmuch sorrow.**

So that on the contrary you may rather forgive him fully and comfort him, (Plummer) The 'ought' supplied by the translators of the AV implies obligation, as though Paul were telling the Corinthians what they *must* do; whereas he tactfully points out the logical sequence of events, leaving them to take the appropriate action. The punishment having proved sufficient to secure the sinner's repentance, this should give place to his immediate reinstatement by the congregation.

lest by any means such a one should be swallowed up by his overmuch sorrow. (Plummer) Otherwise there is a grave danger that he might be overwhelmed with excessive grief. The emphatic placing of 'such a one' at the very end of the sentence gives expression to Paul's compassionate concern for the man. 'The character which Paul here exhibits reflects the image of our heavenly Father. His word is filled with denunciations against impenitent sinners, and at the same time with assurances of unbounded pity and tenderness towards the penitent. He never breaks the bruised reed or quenches the smoking flax.' (Hodge)

V8: **Wherefore I beseech you that ye would confirm your love toward him.**

To prevent the man from falling into hopeless despair, Paul

entreats the Corinthians to assure him of their love by formally receiving 'him again as a brother; and in their forgiveness and welcome he is to find the pledge of the great love of God.' (Denney) ('Confirm' or ratify as in Gal. 3:15)

*V*9: **For to this end also did I write, that I might know the proof of you, whether ye be obedient in all things.**

Another reason for having written 1 Corinthians was to test their obedience to his authority. But as their genuineness was proved by the expulsion of the offender, Paul now has every confidence that the joyful duty of absolving the repentant sinner will command their willing response. For the passing of this crucial test had shown 'that they would be equally obedient in other and lesser cases.' (Lenski)

*V*10: **To whom ye forgive any thing, I forgive also: for if I forgave any thing, to whom I forgave it, for your sakes forgave I it in the person of Christ;**

But to whom ye forgive anything, I forgive also: (RV) Since the forgiveness of the sin must come from the party who is injured by it, the Corinthians must take the lead in this matter, though Paul assures them that their forgiveness of the now repentant offender is also matched by his own.

for what I also have forgiven, if I have forgiven anything, (RV) He 'does not mean that his forgiveness is dubious, or in suspense; what he does is to deprecate the thought that his forgiveness is the main thing, or that he had been the person principally offended.' (Denney)

for your sakes have I forgiven it (RV) Because the sin affected him only as it affected his relations with them, his forgiveness was for *their* sake. Satan was thus denied the advantage he would otherwise have gained. (*v* 11)

in the presence of Christ; (RV margin) Christ is the witness of the sincerity of his forgiveness. 'No man can be severe in his judgment who feels that the mild eyes of Christ are fixed upon him.' (Hodge)

V11: **Lest Satan should get an advantage of us: for we are not ignorant of his devices.**

That no advantage may be gained over us by Satan: (RV) Satan had far more at stake in this affair than the destruction of one sinner. [1 *Cor* 5:5] His scheme was to use this man's offence to introduce a permanent estrangement between the Corinthians and Paul. For if he failed in making Paul embittered towards them, he had hoped to succeed in alienating them from their apostle. But his devices were frustrated, and even the sinner had been snatched from his grasp. (Lenski)

for we are not ignorant of his devices. ' "Ignorant" and "devices" are akin in sound and root [NOEMATA AGNOOUMEN]: we are not without *knowledge* of his *knowing* schemes: here to trip up one by excessive grief, as before by licentiousness: to make not only men's lusts, but their very repentance, his instrument of destruction, under the guise of religion [*Eph* 6:11].' (Fausset)

V12: **Furthermore, when I came to Troas to preach Christ's gospel, and a door was opened unto me of the Lord,**

V13: **I had no rest in my spirit, because I found not Titus my brother: but taking my leave of them, I went from thence into Macedonia.**

Now having come to Troas for the gospel of Christ, and a door having been opened for me in the Lord,

(Lenski) Paul now resumes the account of his movements after leaving Ephesus. [1:8] In accordance with his revised itinerary he travelled to Troas where he not only intended to preach the gospel, but also found a favourable opportunity for doing so while he awaited the return of Titus from Corinth. [cf. *Acts* 14:27; 1 *Cor* 16:9; *Col* 4:3] As Dr P. E. Hughes observes, the expression 'in the Lord' is an evidence of the thoroughly Christocentric nature of Paul's thought: 'The Lord Christ is both the content of the Apostle's message and also the sphere of his opportunity.'

I have had no relief for my spirit because I did not find Titus, my brother, but after taking my leave of them I went forth to Macedonia. (Lenski) When Titus failed to arrive Paul became so anxious about the outcome of the crisis in Corinth that he was unable to continue his work among the people of Troas, and bidding them farewell he crossed over to Macedonia. It was therefore 'a great proof of his very special affection for the Corinthians that his concern for them would not let him rest anywhere, not even in a place that offered great hope of success, till he had news of them.' (Calvin)

*V*14: **Now thanks be unto God, which always causeth us to triumph in Christ, and maketh manifest the savour of his knowledge by us in every place.**

But thanks be unto God, who always leadeth us in triumph in Christ, (ARV) At this point Paul does not stop to explain how his anxiety was relieved by the coming of Titus [7:5ff], but immediately acknowledges his gratitude to God in a jubilant shout of praise. The figure is probably taken from a Roman triumph which the emperor would grant to a victorious general, the glory of whose conquests was also shared by his staff (cf. Bruce: 'Now thanks to God, who always gives us a place of honour in Christ's triumphal procession').

and maketh manifest through us the savour of his knowledge in every place. (RV) This is an extension of the same image, for on such occasions the burning of incense carried the fragrance of victory far and wide. Thus Paul sees his apostolic progress through the world as a continuous triumph, by means of which the knowledge of Christ is spread abroad like perfume. As Christ's loyal lieutenant triumph is assured to Paul 'in every place,' even at Corinth, the place where he had appeared to be facing an ignominious defeat!

*V*15: **For we are unto God a sweet savour of Christ, in them that are saved, and in them that perish:**

*V*16a: **To the one we are the savour of death unto death; and to the other the savour of life unto life.**

As Paul is a chosen vessel filled with the fragrance of Christ, his preaching of the gospel is always a sweet savour to God, no matter whether men 'are being saved' through receiving it, or 'are perishing' in their rejection of it. (RV) The gospel divides mankind into two, and only two classes. In the one it is a fatal aroma that ends in death; in the other, a vital fragrance that leads to life. 'The Gospel is preached unto salvation, for that is its real purpose, but only believers share in this salvation; for unbelievers it is an occasion of condemnation, but it is they who make it so ... The proper function of the Gospel is always to be distinguished from what we may call its accidental function, which must be imputed to the depravity of men by which life is turned into death.' (Calvin)

*V*16b: **And who is sufficient for these things?**

*V*17: **For we are not as many, which corrupt the word of God: but as of sincerity, but as of God, in the sight of God speak we in Christ.**

And for these things who (is) **sufficient?** (Lenski) Since these momentous issues of life and death hang upon the preaching of the gospel, who is competent to exercise such a ministry? Who indeed, if not the apostle himself? [cf. 3:5] Certainly not 'the many' (RV), those false apostles who sought to establish their own authority in the church at Corinth by defaming that of its founder.

For we are not, like so many, peddlers of God's word; (RSV) Paul is adequate for the task, for he is not like those cheap-jacks who adulterate the Word of God and sell it for whatever price they can get. 'It is characteristic of these intruders that they go about hawking or peddling the word of God, cheapening and degrading the message by the illegitimate admixture of foreign elements, judaistic or pagan, as a dishonest merchant adulterates wine with water; they seek only their own gain, irrespective of the effect of their teaching on others and careless of the momentous issues which are at stake.' (P. E. Hughes)

but as of sincerity, but as of God, in the sight of God, speak we in Christ. (RV) This 'completes the inward picture of Paul's preaching. His words spring not from selfish, but from genuine purposes, and from God; and are such words as men speak when sincere and when moved by God. They are spoken in the presence of God and in union with Christ as their encompassing element.' (Beet)

CHAPTER THREE

*V*1: **Do we begin again to commend ourselves? or need we, as some others, epistles of commendation to you, or letters of commendation from you?**

Are we beginning again to commend ourselves? (RV) In thus protesting his sincerity, Paul is well aware that his opponents, whose calumnies had forced him to defend his integrity, would say that he was again indulging a penchant for self-commendation, [e.g. 1 *Cor* 4:16; 9:15; 11:1; 14:18 etc]. [cf. 5:12; 10:18; 13:6]

or need we, as do some, epistles of commendation to you or from you? (RV) But unlike 'some' ('the many' of 2:17), Paul does not think that those whom he has begotten through the gospel will suggest that he needs any introduction to them or any commendation from them. [1 *Cor* 4:15] These false teachers, however, had needed letters of commendation to gain access to the Corinthian church. And they would require similar letters on their departure from it, 'for they were largely dependent on these bills of clearance for profitable marketing of their merchandise in spiritual things.' (P. E. Hughes) What Paul condemns is the unprincipled exploitation of this practice by these men; he has nothing to say against the usefulness of such letters in general. [*Acts* 18:27; *Rom* 16:1; 1 *Cor* 16:3]

V2: **Ye are our epistle written in our hearts, known and read of all men:**

If Paul has no need to flourish any testimonial that could be written with ink, it is because the Corinthians are his credentials. They themselves constitute the 'seal' of his apostleship. [1 *Cor* 9:2] This living letter is not only indelibly inscribed upon his heart [7:3], it is also *recognized* and *read* by everyone. (Bruce) For though outsiders could not inspect Paul's heart, what Christ had written on their heart through his ministry 'was patent to the world's observation, as it was reflected in their Christian mode of life.' (Bernard) [*Matt* 5:14; *Rom* 1:8]

V3: **Forasmuch as ye are manifestly declared to be the epistle of Christ ministered by us, written not with ink, but with the Spirit of the living God, not in tables of stone, but in fleshy tables of the heart.**

Being made manifest that ye are an epistle of Christ, ministered by us, (RV) 'Paul claims no part here but that of Christ's instrument. The Lord, so to speak, dictated the letter, and he wrote it. The contents of it were prescribed by Christ, and through the Apostle's ministry became visible and legible in the Corinthians.' (Denney)

written not with ink, but with the Spirit of the living God; 'This "writing" which the Corinthians exhibit is no writing with ink on a papyrus roll, but is the mystical imprint of the Divine Spirit in their hearts, conveyed through Paul's ministrations.' (Bernard)

not in tables of stone, but in tables that are hearts of

flesh. (RV) The superiority of the new covenant over the old dispensation is not that it sets aside the decalogue (the moral law), but that it transfers that law from tables of stone to 'tables that are hearts of flesh.' This is the fulfilment of Jeremiah's prophecy, 'I will put *my law* in their inward parts, and write it in their hearts.' [*Jer* 31:33] If, as seems likely, Paul's opponents in Corinth were Judaizers who gloried in the law ('ministers of righteousness' 11:15), it is easy to see how the argument of this chapter would fall upon them with overwhelming force It is certain that the original apostles did not endorse this teaching with letters of commendation, but their continued observance of the *ceremonial* law led the Judaizers to suppose 'that legalism was of the essence of their religion.' (J. G. Machen cited by Plummer)

*V*4: **And such trust have we through Christ to God-ward:**

Thus Paul is confident that his work in Corinth is a standing testimony to the reality of his divine commission. 'This confidence is not mere self-assumption, but a firm assurance, reaching through Christ to the presence of God, and therefore valid in the sight of the searcher of hearts.' (Waite)

*V*5: **Not that we are sufficient of ourselves to think any thing as of ourselves; but our sufficiency is of God;**

Not that we are sufficient of ourselves to claim anything as coming from us; our sufficiency is from God, (RSV) But to obviate the charge of boasting Paul at once disclaims any credit for the gracious work that was done in Corinth, for in and of himself he was quite unequal to the task. The secret of his successful ministry there is not to be found in any natural competence, but solely in the sufficiency of the God who called and equipped him for it. [1 *Cor* 15:10; 2 *Cor* 4:7]

*V*6: **Who also hath made us able ministers of the new testament; not of the letter, but of the spirit: for the letter killeth, but the spirit giveth life.**

Who also made us sufficient as ministers of a new covenant; (R v) Instead of believing the empty claims of the false apostles, the Corinthians should be the first to acknowledge that Paul has a valid and effective ministry. It is *valid* because he did not appoint himself to it, but can point to the particular occasion when God's commission made him sufficient for it. [*Acts* 9:3ff ; 22:12ff ; 26:15–18] It is *effective* because it is the ministry of a new covenant. The very provision of a fresh covenant indicates its superiority over the worn out and obsolete dispensation which it replaces. [*Heb* 8:6–13] This covenant is not a mutual compact between equals, but a 'unilateral enactment' of which God is the sovereign disposer; and its uniqueness lies in the accomplishing of that which the law demanded but gave no power to perform.

not of the letter, but of the spirit: for the letter killeth, but the spirit giveth life. The law of God externally engraved on tables of stone is here adversely compared with that same law internally inscribed in the heart of the believer. Sinners confronted by a condemning code could only be killed by it, but the spiritual application of a fulfilled law confers life. Paul neither deprecates the law nor contradicts its plain meaning; he is showing that the natural man's inability to obey it must result in death. [*Rom* 6:23; 7:6–12; *Gal* 3:10] The grace of the new covenant 'is life-giving, in that Christ, who as God is the law-giver and as Man is the *only* law-keeper, vicariously endured the sinner's death penalty, ridding us, as it were, of the legal document with its accusing ordinances and nailing it to His cross for all to see [*Col* 2:14f.], and also, by the Pentecostal outpouring of the Holy Spirit, communicated His life and obedience to every trusting heart.' (P. E. Hughes)

*V*7: **But if the ministration of death, written and engraven in stones, was glorious, so that the children of Israel could not stedfastly behold the face of Moses for the glory of his countenance; which glory was to be done away:**

*V*8: **How shall not the ministration of the spirit be rather glorious?**

As Moses descended from the mount his face shone with a glory that testified to the divine origin of the covenant of which he was the mediator, yet death was the unavoidable result of a ministry whose content was only 'engraved in letters on stones.' (Lenski) [*Exod* 34:29–35] But though the ministration of condemnation was so gloriously inaugurated, the fading of this radiance from the face of Moses showed that its glory 'was being done away.' (RV margin) For God always intended to replace it with the abiding and far more resplendent ministration of the spirit. Nevertheless it is the function of the law to convict men of their sin and drive them to faith in the promise. [*Gal* 3:24; 25] Consequently even the Old Testament saints were saved by their faith in the promise, and not by their obedience to the law. [*Rom* 4:1–8] For 'by the deeds of the law there shall no flesh be justified in his sight.' [*Rom* 3:20; *Gal* 2:16] In effect Paul warns the Corinthians that to give heed to Judaizers who exalt the law at the expense of the gospel is to turn away from that salvation which is theirs by grace through faith alone.

*V*9: **For if the ministration of condemnation be glory,**

much more doth the ministration of righteousness exceed in glory.

The ministration of righteousness abounds with greater glory than that which attended the ministry of condemnation, for it is a greater matter to secure the justification of a sinner than to confirm his condemnation. It takes only the letter of the law on slabs of stone to condemn him, but it required the blood of God's own Son and the Spirit's quickening power to make him the heir of an everlasting righteousness. (Lenski) [cf. *Rom* 3:19–26; 8:16ff; 1 *Cor* 1:30]

*V*10: **For even that which was made glorious had no glory in this respect, by reason of the glory that excelleth.**

For that which hath been made glorious, hath not been made glorious in this respect, on account of the surpassing glory. (Bernard) Although the ministration of the old covenant was truly glorious, yet this seemed as nothing in comparison with the transcendent glory of the new covenant. 'Just as the moon and the stars, though they are themselves bright and spread their light over all the earth, yet vanish before the greater brightness of the sun, so the Law, however glorious in itself, has no glory in face of the Gospel's grandeur.' (Calvin)

*V*11: **For if that which is done away was glorious, much more that which remaineth is glorious.**

For if that which is being done away was with glory, much more that which remaineth is in glory. (RV margin) At Sinai the old covenant came *with* glory; the new abides *in* glory as its distinctive element. 'The old dispensation and its ministry were temporary, the new is permanent. There is nothing to intervene, no new revelation, no new economy, between the gospel and its ministry, and the final consummation. Whoever are to be converted, whatever nations are to be brought in, it must be by the preaching of the gospel, "which remaineth," or is to continue, according to Christ's promise, until the end of the world.' (Hodge)

*V*12: **Seeing then that we have such hope, we use great plainness of speech:**

Having, therefore, such hope, we continue using full openness of speech, (Lenski) Since Paul has a sure hope that the glory of the new covenant will abide forever (*v* 11), he uses great boldness of speech. For now the full openness of the gospel has superseded the comparative obscurity of the preparatory dispensation. Therefore the unreserved frankness with which he glorifies his ministry is entirely appropriate, even though some should mistake it for self-commendation. (*v* 1) (Massie)

*V*13: **And not as Moses, which put a vail over his face, that the children of Israel could not stedfastly look to the end of that which is abolished:**

And are not as Moses, who put a veil upon his face, that the children of Israel should not look stedfastly unto the end of that which was being done away: (RV margin) As the minister of a covenant whose glory can never be dimmed, it is not for Paul to do as Moses did. [*Exod* 34:33-35 RV] For after Moses had spoken the words of God to the people it was his custom to cover his face with a veil which meant that the Israelites could not even look upon the reflected glory of a vanishing order without concealment. No such intervening veil obscures the clarity of the revelation vouchsafed to Paul. 'His is not a message of condemnation and death, but of grace and mercy and life to every sinner who repents and believes.

[43]

The eye of faith may gaze upon the everlasting glory of Christ without interruption.' (P. E. Hughes)

V14: But their minds were blinded: for until this day remaineth the same vail untaken away in the reading of the old testament; which vail is done away in Christ.

But their minds were blinded: The veil which hid the face of Moses answered to the spiritual insensibility of those to whom he ministered. [*Deut* 29:4] 'Unless God give sight as well as light, and enlighten both organ and object, we can see nothing.' (Trapp)

for until this very day at the reading of the old covenant the same veil remaineth unlifted (for it is *only* done away in Christ). (Bernard) Exactly the same veil of unbelief prevents the Jews of Paul's day from understanding the real significance of the revelation that was given to them through Moses. And it is only by receiving the One of whom Moses spoke that this veil can ever be removed. [*John* 5:46] 'The Old Testament Scriptures are intelligible only when understood as predicting and prefiguring Christ.' (Hodge) (*Luke* 24:44f] Paul here affords striking evidence of his complete dissociation of Judaism from Christianity by describing the religious system of his own early manhood as the 'worn out' (PALAIOS) covenant, especially when it is remembered that it had only been superseded by the new (KAINOS: cf. *v* 6) covenant thirty years before he wrote this letter. (Bernard) [*Acts* 13:19; *Rom* 10:1ff; *Phil* 3:3ff]

V15: But even unto this day, when Moses is read, the vail is upon their heart.

But unto this day, whensoever Moses is read, a veil lieth upon their heart. (RV) The thought of the previous verse is here carried to its climax. As the veil over Moses' face concealed the passing glory of the old covenant, so today their descendants fail to understand the Book of Moses, even though it is read to them every Sabbath. [*Acts* 15:21] 'Like its author at Sinai, the book is veiled. Or, rather, on the readers' hearts a veil lies. For the hindrance is in themselves.' (Beet)

*V*16: **Nevertheless when it shall turn to the Lord, the vail shall be taken away.**

But, whensoever a man shall turn to the Lord, at once the veil is taken away. (Plummer) Although Moses veiled his face before the people, whenever he went in before the Lord he took off the veil 'so that he beheld with unimpeded vision the divine glory.' (P. E. Hughes) [*Exod* 34:34] In the same way, whenever a Jew turns to the Lord (i.e. Christ) the veil of unbelief is taken away from his heart (by God) [cf. *Acts* 9:5, 20]

*V*17: **Now the Lord is that Spirit: and where the Spirit of the Lord is, there is liberty.**

Now the 'Lord' means the 'Spirit'; (Bruce) The spiritual transformation which Paul sees prefigured in the passage just quoted is effected by the Lord who is the Spirit. (*v* 18) In thus virtually identifying the exalted Christ with the Holy Spirit, the apostle is not confusing the distinct identity of their persons, but is stressing the unity of their work in the economy of redemption. For as every genuine experience of the Spirit must lead to the confession 'Jesus is Lord' [1 *Cor* 12:3], so here Paul insists 'that what the Spirit does is exactly what the Lord does; the Spirit's work is not an additional or special work *beyond* the Lord's; the Spirit *is* the Lord at work.' (F. D. Bruner, *A Theology of the Holy Spirit*, p. 289) [cf. *John* 16:12–16]

and where the Spirit of the Lord is, there is liberty. It is always and only by His Spirit that Christ communicates to men the liberty He died to secure, so that whenever He removes the veil of unbelief from their hearts the bondage of the law gives way to the freedom of the gospel. [*John* 8:36, 39; *Gal* 5:1]

*V*18: **But we all, with open face beholding as in a glass the glory of the Lord, are changed into the same image from glory to glory, even as by the Spirit of the Lord.**

But we all, with unveiled face beholding as in a mirror the glory of the Lord, (ARV) Whereas Moses alone was privileged to behold the glory of God with unveiled face, now all Christians may always gaze directly upon the full revelation of that glory 'in the face of Jesus Christ.' [4:6] 'We are transformed into the image of the Lord by beholding it, not by reflecting it. The common interpretation is therefore to be preferred; *beholding as in a mirror.* Though in comparison with the unconverted those who are turned to the Lord see clearly, or with an unveiled face, still it is only as in a mirror. 1 *Cor* 13:12. It is not the immediate, beatific vision of the glory of the Lord, which is only enjoyed in heaven, but it is that manifestation of his glory which is made in his word and by his Spirit, whose office it is to glorify Christ by revealing him to us. John 16:14.' (Hodge)

are being changed into his likeness from one degree of glory to another; (RSV) There are indeed many who wish to find a short-cut to glory, but only those who continually behold the glory of Christ in the mirror of His word know anything of this progressive transformation 'into the same image.' [*Prov* 4:18]

for this comes from the Lord who is the Spirit. (RSV)

[46]

Once more Paul emphatically rejects that spurious spirituality which would sever the work of the Spirit from the Lord whose mission He fulfils in the world. (*v* 17) 'Our whole transformation is the work of the Lord in and by and through the Spirit. All Scripture agrees in regard to that.' (Lenski)

CHAPTER FOUR

*V*1: **Therefore seeing we have this ministry, as we have received mercy, we faint not;**

Therefore seeing we have this ministry, even as we obtained mercy, we faint not: (RV) It is not in any spirit of self-sufficiency, but with a lively sense of the distinguishing mercy of God in granting this glorious ministry of the New Covenant to one who 'was before a blasphemer and a persecutor' that Paul continues faith.ully to discharge it despite all discouragements. [*Exod* 33:19; 1 *Tim* 1:12–16] As the unworthy recipient of such mercy and such a ministry he does not lose heart, remaining resolute in his refusal to compromise the truth of the gospel to suit Jewish prejudice. [*v* 2ff; *Gal* 5:11; 6:12]

*V*2: **But have renounced the hidden things of dishonesty, not walking in craftiness, nor handling the word of God deceitfully; but by manifestation of the truth commending ourselves to every man's conscience in the sight of God.**

But we have renounced the things that are hidden out of a sense of shame, (Arndt-Gingrich) As befits the openness of his ministry, Paul has refused to adopt the tactics of the false apostles who gain their converts by guile, and who try to hide their shame by accusing him of the very thing of which they themselves are guilty. [12:16]

not walking in craftiness, nor handling the word of God deceitfully; The apostle plainly contrasts the purity of his own conduct and his honest proclamation of the Word of God with the deceitful practice of these interlopers who robbed the gospel of its power to save by their adulteration of its content in order to enrich themselves. [2:17]

but by manifestation of the truth commending ourselves to every man's conscience On the contrary, Paul's ministry is marked by 'the open proclamation of the truth' (Arndt-Gingrich), and it is solely by this transparent fidelity to 'the whole counsel of God' that he expects to commend himself (lit.) 'to every conscience of men.' For he is confident that the truth, the whole truth, and nothing but the truth, must find an answering echo in every conscience, even if it be sinfully suppressed by many.

in the sight of God This is added 'because conscience holds us accountable to God. Drop the idea of God, and the vitality of conscience is destroyed. Mere abstract ideas of "right" and "wrong" do not bind the conscience; the idea of God and his judgment does.' (Lenski) [1:12; 2:17]

V3 : But if our gospel be hid, it is hid to them that are lost:

But and if our gospel is veiled, it is veiled in them that are perishing: (RV) The fact that the unveiled glory of the gospel preached by Paul remains hidden from many is their condemnation, and marks them out as those who are on the high road to perdition. 'Those from whom it is hidden must therefore be blind and lacking in every trace of rational understanding. The conclusion is that the blindness of unbelievers in no way detracts from the clarity of his Gospel;

the sun is no less bright because blind men do not perceive its light.' (Calvin)

*V*4: **In whom the god of this world hath blinded the minds of them which believe not, lest the light of the glorious gospel of Christ, who is the image of God, should shine unto them.**

In whom the god of this age hath blinded the minds of the unbelieving, (RV margin) It is because Satan has blinded their minds that those who are perishing do not believe the only Word that could save them. And it is by this blinding of the mind that Satan has secured their vassalage to himself as 'the god of this age,' though as dependent creatures neither he nor they ever succeed in escaping from the lordship and judgment of the one living and true God. As Trapp observes, 'The devil usurps such a power, and wicked men will have it so ... Their buildings, ploughings, plantings, sailings, are for the devil. And if we could rip up their hearts, we should find written therein, The god of this present world.' [*John* 12:31; 16:11; *Eph* 2:2; 1 *John* 5:19]

that they should not see the light of the gospel of the glory of Christ, (RV margin) Unlike the message peddled by the Judaizers, Paul's gospel is a revelation of the glory of Christ. [*Acts* 26:13–18] 'To see this glory is to be saved; for we are thereby transformed into his likeness from glory to glory, 3:18. Therefore it is that Satan, the great adversary, directs all his energy to prevent men becoming the subjects of that illumination of which the gospel, as the revelation of the glory of Christ, is the source.' (Hodge)

who is the image of God. 'He who sees the Son, sees the Father, *in the face* of Christ. The Son exactly represents and reflects the Father.' (Bengel) [*John* 14:9; *Heb* 1:3]

*V*5: **For we preach not ourselves, but Christ Jesus the Lord; and ourselves your servants for Jesus' sake.**

For we preach not ourselves, but Christ Jesus as Lord, (RV) Since Paul was commissioned to preach a gospel which has the glory of Christ for its content, he does not preach himself as his opponents allege, but Christ Jesus as Lord. Hence those who reject his preaching, repudiate not the preacher but the Christ he preaches. 'To "preach Christ as Lord" is to preach Him as crucified, risen, and glorified, the Lord to whom "all authority in heaven and earth has been given." To confess Him as Lord is to declare oneself a Christian [*Rom* 10:9; 1 *Cor* 12:3].' (Plummer)

and ourselves as your servants for Jesus' sake. (RV) Far from claiming any lordship over their faith [1:24], Paul presents himself as their bondservant for the sake of the one Master 'who took upon him the form of a servant.' [*Phil* 2:7] Thus though he is their minister, they are not his masters. [1 *Cor* 7:23] 'The ideal of a Christian minister, as presented in this pregnant passage, is, that he is a preacher of Christ, and a servant of the church, governed and animated by the love of Jesus.' (Hodge)

*V*6: **For God, who commanded the light to shine out of darkness, hath shined in our hearts, to give the light of the knowledge of the glory of God in the face of Jesus Christ.**

Seeing it is God, that said, Light shall shine out of darkness, who shined in our hearts, to give the light of the knowledge of the glory of God in the face of Jesus Christ. (RV) Paul cannot but preach Christ, for God whose first creative word brought light out of darkness [*Gen* 1:3], is He who shone into his heart in re-creating grace. [5:17] As this spiritual experience is common to all Christians, Paul here stresses the subjective effect of this ('in our hearts') instead of dwelling upon the objective vision of Christ by which it was produced in him. [1 Cor 9:1] 'For as in His creation of the world God has poured forth upon us the brightness of the sun and has also given us eyes with which to receive it, so in our redemption He shines forth upon us in the person of His Son by His Gospel, but that would be in vain, since we are blind, unless He were also to illuminate our minds by His Spirit.' (Calvin) Moreover, it is only because Paul has been divinely illuminated himself that he can be used by God to turn men 'from darkness to light.' [Acts 26:18] For those whose spiritual eyes are still covered by the scales of unbelief obviously cannot reveal Christ to others. [cf. Acts 9:18]

V7: But we have this treasure in earthen vessels, that the excellency of the power may be of God, and not of us.

After Paul has spoken so exultantly of 'the light of the knowledge of the glory of God' (v 6), it is surprising to find that this treasure is placed in such mean and perishable vessels. The 'majesty of the message is in strange contrast with the weak and buffeted and fragile person of the messenger.' (Menzies) [Job 4:19; 2 Cor 10:10; 12:7]

that the exceeding greatness of the power may be God's and not from ourselves. (Bernard) The amazing effects produced by the possession of this divine knowledge are evidently 'beyond all measure and proportion' to the means used to diffuse it. (Arndt-Gingrich) For it is God's purpose to show that this power cannot be ascribed to the weak vessels in which it is contained, but that it belongs continually to Him from whom it comes. (Fausset) (12:9)

V8: We are troubled on every side, yet not distressed; we are perplexed, but not in despair;

*V*9: **Persecuted, but not forsaken; cast down, but not destroyed;**

Paul's constant experience as a minister of Christ is now illustrated in a vivid metaphor, expressed in four pairs of participles which form a climax. 'The first clause in each member of the series implies the *earthiness of the vessels*, the second clause the *excellency of the power.*' (Fausset)

1. **In every direction pressed hard, but not hemmed in;** (Bernard) The Apostle thinks of himself as a combatant engaged by an apparently stronger foe whose persistent attacks leave him no room to manoeuvre, yet God does not suffer him to be crushed into a corner. [1 *Cor* 10:13]

2. **bewildered, but not utterly despairing;** (Bernard) Or preserving the play on words: 'confused, but not confounded.' (P. E. Hughes) He is often perplexed by the crafty stratagems of his adversary, but God does not permit him to be reduced to blank despair. [1:8-10; 7:5ff.]

3. **pursued, but not forsaken** (i.e. abandoned to the pursuing foe); (Bernard) Although he is hunted by a killer intent on dealing him the death-blow, he is not deserted by God in his extremity. [*Heb* 13:5]

4. **struck down** (as by an arrow), **but not destroyed.** (Bernard) And even when he is felled by what his enemy takes to be the final stroke, the unexpected power of God ensures that he is far from finished. [*Acts* 14:19f.; 2 *Cor* 11:23]

*V*10: **Always bearing about in the body the dying of the Lord Jesus, that the life also of Jesus might be made manifest in our body.**

Always bearing about in the body the putting to death of Jesus, (RV margin) This sums up and explains the significance of the apostle's sufferings, [*vv* 8, 9] His devotion to Jesus is the magnet that irresistibly draws the world's hostility upon himself. [*Gal* 6:17] For the same enmity which reached its culmination in the crucifixion of Jesus now pursues those whom He has chosen out of the world. [*John* 15:18-21] The verse shows that Paul 'taught his converts details in the history of Jesus, especially His sufferings ending in death. Here he assumes that they know.' (Plummer)

that the life also of Jesus may be manifested in our body. (RV) This discloses the purpose of these sufferings. Paul bears about the *dying* of Jesus in order that the *life* also of Jesus may be manifested in his body. For the inextinguishable resurrection-life of the Jesus who once died is demonstrated in his many deliverances from the jaws of death. It is evident that the distinction made by liberal theologians between the 'Jesus of history' and the 'Christ of faith' was quite foreign to Paul's thought. He 'does not separate the historic Jesus from the glorified Christ. To him it is the same Jesus.' (Plummer)

*V*11: **For we which live are alway delivered unto death for Jesus' sake, that the life also of Jesus might be made manifest in our mortal flesh.**
Several new elements appear in this explanatory re-statement of the previous verse. 1. It is because Paul is a 'living one,' i.e. one whose essential life is the eternal life of Jesus, that the deaths to which he is always being handed over serve to exhibit the triumph of that divine life. 2. The sphere in which this resurrection-life of Jesus is displayed is a body of 'mortal flesh,' i.e. a body in subjection to the power of death. 'Christ's followers are in this life delivered unto death, that His life may be manifested in that which naturally is the seat of decay and death. That which is subject to suffering is that in which the power of Him who suffered here is most manifested.' (Vine) 3. 'It is for Jesus' sake – because of Jesus – that he suffers. It is only suffering of this kind, which is so abundantly blessed.' (Goudge)

*V*12: **So then death worketh in us, but life in you.**

Although Paul knows that death is already at work in him, he is comforted by the fact that his *physical* sufferings have been fruitful in bringing *spiritual* life to the Corinthians. 'In other words, Paul is reminding them again that he, who through many afflictions brought them this transforming message, is their genuine Apostle.' (P. E. Hughes)

*V*13: **We having the same spirit of faith, according as it is written, I believed, and therefore have I spoken; we also believe, and therefore speak;**

But having the same spirit of faith, according to that which is written, I believed, and therefore did I speak; we also believe, and therefore also we speak; (RV) Since Paul has the same spirit of faith as David had in similar straits ('I believed, and therefore did I speak': *Ps* 116:10), he also believes and continues to declare his faith, even though death should soon silence his testimony to the truth. [cf. *Acts* 4:20] This means that Paul and David share the same objective faith. For both testaments contain the same truth, the Old in the form of promise, the New in the form of fulfilment. 'Hence the spirit of both is identical in defying persecution and death.' (Lenski)

*V*14: **Knowing that he which raised up the Lord Jesus shall raise up us also by Jesus, and shall present us with you.**

Paul is fearless in the face of death because he knows that God who raised up the Lord Jesus 'shall raise up us also *with* Jesus.' (RV) This obviously does not mean at the same time as Jesus, but in virtue of our union with Him. For there could be no resurrection of believers apart from His triumph over death.

[1 *Cor* 15:23] And God will raise up Paul together with the believers in Corinth ('us with you') in order to present them 'before the presence of his glory with exceeding joy.' [11:2; *Col* 1:22; *Eph* 5:27; *Jude* 24] Because Paul here speaks of being raised from the dead, some have maintained that this represents a change in his eschatological expectations [cf. 1 *Thess* 4:15, 17]. But it is a mistake to assume that the exhortation to live in the light of the imminent return of Christ was based on a categorical assurance that either he or his immediate readers (in Thessalonica, or elsewhere) would be alive when that event took place.

In this respect Paul knew no more than we do ourselves today, for neither the time of his death nor the date of the Parousia was revealed to him. (Lenski) [*Matt* 24:36]

*V*15: **For all things are for your sakes, that the abundant grace might through the thanksgiving of many redound to the glory of God.**

For all things are for your sakes, Hence the proximate end of Paul's sufferings (*vv* 7-13) is the salvation of the Corinthians, while the ultimate result is the glory of God.

that the grace, being multiplied through the many, may cause thanksgiving to abound unto the glory of God. (RV) This means that 'the more people who come to know the grace of God through the gospel Paul preaches, the more numerous will be the thanksgivings that will be evoked, and the greater the praise that will be offered to God.' (Tasker)

*V*16: **For which cause we faint not; but though our outward man perish, yet the inward man is renewed day by day.**

Wherefore we faint not; (RV) Buoyed up by this resurrection hope (*v* 14) it is no wonder that Paul does not lose heart. (Plummer) (cf. *v* 1)

on the contrary, even if our outer man is being destroyed, nevertheless our inner one is being renewed day by day. (Lenski) As the contrast Paul makes here is between the declining powers of his bodily life and the progressive renewal of his spiritual life, the 'outer man' must not be confused with the unregenerate 'old man' of *Rom* 6:6; *Eph* 4:22 and *Col* 3:9. It is evident that the apostle's afflictions have hastened that process of decay to which his physical life, as at present constituted, is subject. This necessarily includes every faculty which depends upon the body for its proper functioning. On the other hand, what he most essentially *is* by regenerating grace cannot be destroyed, but is being renewed day by day. [3:18] 'The decay of the outward man in the godless is a melancholy spectacle, for it is the decay of everything; in the Christian it does not touch that life which is hid with Christ in God, and which is in the soul itself a well of water springing up to life eternal.' (Denney) [*John* 4:14; *Col* 3:3]

*V*17: **For our light affliction, which is but for a moment, worketh for us a far more exceeding and eternal weight of glory;**

For our present light burden of affliction worketh out for us more and more exceedingly an eternal heavy burden of glory; (Bernard) As the verb 'worketh' also means 'earns,' Roman Catholic expositors use the verse as a text on which to hang their doctrine of merit. But though God makes present afflictions the means of obtaining future glory, it is false to infer that they are the meritorious cause of it. 'The spirit of faith which realizes the substance of things not seen inverts the usual relation of ideas. Affliction, generally regarded as a load, has here the quality of lightness. Glory, generally regarded as an ethereal splendour, is a weight. The affliction is not light in itself, but only when put in the balance with the weight, nor momentary in itself, but only when set against eternity . . . The idea in the Apostle's mind is that the sufferings of Christ borne by his ministers and followers lead them to glory, even as they led Christ Himself to glory, because they are always accompanied by rich supplies of the Spirit and life.' (Waite) [*Rom* 8:17, 18]

V18: **While we look not at the things which are seen, but at the things which are not seen: for the things which are seen are temporal; but the things which are not seen are eternal.**

Meanwhile Paul fixes his gaze not on the things seen but on the things not seen: for the things which are visible to the eye of sense are transient, but the realities which as yet can only be discerned by the eye of faith are eternal. 'Note well what it is that will make all the miseries of this world easy to endure; it is that we should transfer our thoughts to the eternity of the kingdom of heaven. If we look around us, a moment can seem a long time, but when we lift up our hearts heavenwards, a thousand years begin to be like a moment.' (Calvin)

CHAPTER FIVE

V1: For we know that if our earthly house of this tabernacle were dissolved, we have a building of God, an house not made with hands, eternal in the heavens.

For we know that Paul is lifted above earthly affliction by this heavenly hope. [4:17, 18] For he knows by immediate revelation, as the Corinthians also know because he had taught it them [1 *Cor* 15], that when the frail tent in which they live their earthly life is dismantled by death, they 'have a building from God, a house not made with hands, eternal, in the heavens.' It is only the certainty of the resurrection of the body to life eternal that enables him to contemplate its dissolution with composure.

if 'The reason why Paul treats this as only a possibility and not an inevitability is because it is balanced by another possibility, namely, that of the prior return of Christ, in which case he will not experience death, but immediate bodily translation and transformation.' (P. E. Hughes) (See also comment on 4:14)

the earthly tent we live in is taken down, (Arndt-Gingrich) Those who know that they have no permanent place on earth are content with such a temporary dwelling until they reach that city 'which hath foundations, whose builder and maker is God.' [*Heb* 11:10] 'The camp-life of the Israelites in the

wilderness, as commemorated by the annual feast of Taber-
nacles, was a ready and appropriate symbol of man's transitory
life on earth: while the land of promise with its settled abodes,
the land flowing with milk and honey, typified the eternal
inheritance of the redeemed.' (Lightfoot on Phil 1:23, cited
by P. E. Hughes) [Lev 23:42]

we have The present tense expresses the certainty of our
possessing it, and must not be pressed to suggest 'the mechanical
theory that the body of glory exists *now* in heaven, in an organic
form.' (Waite)

**a building from God, a house not made with hands,
eternal,** (RV) The body of the future will be 'not made with
hands' [cf. *Col* 2:11; *Heb* 9:11], for it is the direct creation of
God, an eternal building as contrasted with a perishable tent.
[1 *Cor* 15:38] From this it would appear certain that Paul knew
of the charge that was brought against the Lord, that he would
destroy the temple made with hands, and in three days build
another 'not made with hands.' (Goudge) [*Mark* 14:58; cf.
John 2:19–21]

in the heavens. 'It is practically in heaven: for the power
which will raise it is there. When Christ appears from heaven
we shall receive our permanent bodily abode. Hence it is also
"our dwelling place from heaven," v.2. Consequently, this
building is completely beyond reach of the uncertainties of
earth.' (Beet)

*V*2: **For in this we groan, earnestly desiring to be clothed
upon with our house which is from heaven:**

For in the meantime indeed we groan, (P. E. Hughes)
'If Paul had no hope, he would not sigh for the future; but the
very longing which pressed the sighs from his bosom became

itself a witness to the glory which awaited him . . . The spiritual instincts are prophetic. They have not been implanted in the soul by God only to be disappointed.' (Denney) [*Rom* 8:23]

longing to be clothed upon with our habitation (RV) '*lit.* "to have it put on over" the earthly body, so that there shall be transformation [1 *Cor* 15:51 *f.*), not death.' (Massie)

which is from heaven: The 'distinguishing properties of the resurrection-body will be the efflux of that resurrection-life which resides in "the Lord from heaven." And, as Bengel says, if it be "*from* heaven," the thing meant cannot be heaven itself.' (Brown)

*V*3: **If so be that being clothed we shall not be found naked.**

Inasmuch as we, having put it on, shall not be found naked. (Arndt-Gingrich) This clarifies and confirms the meaning of the previous verse. If Paul is still clothed with his natural body at the Lord's appearing, he will avoid the nakedness of the disembodied state. For then 'his assumption of the new body will be a superinvestment, a process like that of putting on an upper garment.' (Waite)

*V*4: **For we that are in this tabernacle do groan, being burdened: not for that we would be unclothed, but clothed upon, that mortality might be swallowed up of life.**

We that are in the tent do groan being burdened, because we would not be unclothed, but be clothed upon, (Vos) The burden under which Paul groans is not the mere fear of death, but the separation of the body from the soul by death. Because death is the unnatural disruption of man's being as created by God, he could never be satisfied with a gospel which only provided for the redemption of the soul. He longs for something far richer than the bodiless survival of the soul after death. What therefore concerns him is whether he will have to face 'a *protracted* state of being unclothed, that is "naked" between his possible death and the arrival of the parousia?' (Vos) For he cannot regard his salvation as complete until he is clothed with the resurrection-body of glory.

that what is mortal may be swallowed up of life. (RV) Thus Paul would prefer to be alive at Christ's coming so that his present mortal body might immediately be transformed into the body of glory. [1 *Cor* 15:53, 54]

*V*5: **Now he that hath wrought us for the selfsame thing is God, who also hath given unto us the earnest of the Spirit.**

Now he that wrought us for this very thing is God, (RV) This 'groaning for glory' is the very thing 'for which God has prepared the believer, which He causes to issue from his heart, whence also it has a prophetic significance, becomes a confirmation of the assurance that he shall obtain the heavenly body.' (Vos) (v.2)

who gave unto us the earnest of the Spirit. (RV) The present possession of the Spirit is the specific pledge of this future life. 'The Spirit's proper sphere is the future aeon; from thence He projects Himself into the present, and becomes a prophecy of Himself in His eschatological operations.' (Vos) [1:22; *Rom* 8-11; *Eph* 1:14]

*V*6: **Therefore we are always confident, knowing that, whilst we are at home in the body, we are absent from the Lord:**

Being therefore always of good courage, and knowing that, whilst we are at home in the body, we are absent from the Lord (RV) Paul is always of good courage, despite his uncertainty as to whether he will be still in the body when the parousia takes place, for he knows that as long as he stays in this earthly tent, he is away from that heavenly home which is with His glorified Lord. Although Christ is always *spiritually* present with His people, He is *physically* absent from them while they remain on earth. Now 'He does not show Himself to us face to face, because we are still exiles from His kingdom and do not yet possess that blessed immortality that the angels who are with Him enjoy.' (Calvin)

V7: **(For we walk by faith, not by sight:)**

The parenthesis explains the sense in which Paul is 'absent from the Lord.' For while he is at home in the body, the region 'through which he walks is one in which the heavenly things gazed upon are not seen in their actual substance, but only realized, as far as that is possible, by the spiritual discernment of faith [*Heb* 11:1]. When he migrates to the Lord, he enjoys the sight of the things themselves.' (Waite)

V8: **We are confident, I say, and willing rather to be absent from the body, and to be present with the Lord.**

We are of good courage, I say, and are willing rather to be absent from the body, and to be at home with the Lord. (RV) Since Paul was unsure of what was in store for him, 'he says only as much as he could with full certainty profess: to be absent from the body is to be at home with the Lord. Even in case that happened which appeared to him the less desirable, he would still be contented, because in this being with the Lord everything else was potentially given.' (Vos) [cf. *Phil* 1:21–23]

*V*9: **Wherefore we labour, that, whether present or absent, we may be accepted of him.**

Wherefore also we make it our aim, whether at home or absent, to be well-pleasing unto him. (RV) Whether therefore Paul is in the body or out of it at the Lord's return, his constant ambition, and the only lawful one (Bengel), is to win His approval. For whatever the Lord's appointment for him may be, whether it be life or death, his absolute commitment to Christ remains the same. [*Rom* 14:8; *Phil* 1:20; 1 *Thess* 5:10]

*V*10: **For we must all appear before the judgment seat of Christ; that every one may receive the things done in his body, according to that he hath done, whether it be good or bad.**

For Paul makes it his aim to be well-pleasing to Christ because he is to be judged by Christ, and so are the hypercritical Corinthians!

we must all 'Though this is something that applied to all men, all men do not have minds sufficiently exalted to remember every single moment that they must appear before the judgment-seat of Christ.' (Calvin) Paul speaks of the one general judgment of all men by Christ, before whose tribunal even Christians must stand. 'It is impossible to identify a series of distinct and separate judgments.' (G. E. Ladd, 'Eschatology,' *The New Bible Dictionary*, p. 389) [cf. *Matt* 25:31–46; *John* 12:48; *Acts* 17:30, 31; *Rom* 2:16; 2 *Tim* 4:1; 2 *Pet* 3:7]

be made manifest (RV) 'We are at all times "manifest" to God; *then* we shall be so to the assembled intelligent universe and to ourselves; for the judgment shall be not only in order to assign the everlasting portion to each, but to vindicate God's righteousness, so that it shall be manifest to all His creatures, and even to the sinner himself.' (Fausset)

before the judgment seat of Christ; 'The Judge on this great occasion is to be, not God absolutely considered, but the God-man in his office as mediatorial King. All judgment is said to be, not inherently his, but *committed* to him by the Father. *John* 5:22, 27.' (A. A. Hodge, *The Confession of Faith*, p. 390)

in order that each one may *receive as his due* **the things done by means of his body,** (Plummer) All men are to be judged, but not in the mass. For each man will be individually assessed so that 'there will be exact correspondence between action and requital.' (Theodoret cited by Plummer)

according to what he hath done, (RV) 'The gospel teaches us that while believers are not rewarded on account of their works, they are rewarded according to their works.' For 'while our works are naught as a ground of merit for justification, they are all-important as evidences that we are justified.' (R. L. Dabney, 'The Moral Effects of a Free Justification': *Discussions*, Vol. 1, pp. 86, 89) [cf. 11:15; *Rom* 2:6; *Rev* 20:12]

whether it be good or whether it be worthless. (P. E. Hughes) 'The change to the neuter singular is significant. It seems to imply that, although persons will be judged one by one and not in groups, yet conduct in each case will be judged as a whole. In other words, it is character rather than separate acts that will be rewarded or punished . . . It is habitual action that will be judged. And this explains the aorist; it is what he did during his lifetime that is summed up and estimated as a total. Human tribunals deal with crime; they have punishments, but no rewards. The Divine tribunal has both.' (Plummer) [*John* 5:29]

*V*11: **Knowing therefore the terror of the Lord, we persuade men; but we are made manifest unto God; and I trust also are made manifest in your consciences.**

Knowing therefore the fear of the Lord, we persuade men, (RV) The purity of Paul's motives in preaching the gospel is guaranteed by the awe which this forthcoming judgment inspires in him. He is prompted to persuade men by the supreme desire faithfully to discharge the Lord's commission and not by any spirit of self-interest. In fact it is only as a man is imbued with this integrity towards God that his preaching can have any real appeal to men, for those who are not faithful to God are never genuine with men.

but we are made manifest unto God; The *manifestation* of 'the last judgment, ver. 10, has as good as taken place – for God.' (Denney)

and I hope that we are made manifest also in your consciences. (RV) 'Their consciences, rather than their intellects, on which they prided themselves: *conscience penetrates further than the judgment of the flesh*; conscience goes deeper than criticism (Calvin). Paul says "consciences" and not "conscience," because he appeals to the individual conscience of each of them: *the plural has greater weight* (Bengel).' (Plummer)

*V*12: **For we commend not ourselves again unto you, but give you occasion to glory on our behalf, that ye may have somewhat to answer them which glory in appearance, and not in heart.**

We are not again commending ourselves unto you, but speak as giving you occasion of glorying on our behalf, (RV) In thus defending his ministry Paul is not again indulging

CHAPTER 5 VERSES 13-14

in the self-praise with which he was charged by his cynical critics in Corinth. [3:1] But that it should have proved necessary for their father in Christ to supply them with the ammunition to repel these slanders was indeed a reproach to the Corinthians.

that ye may have wherewith to answer them that glory in appearance, and not in heart. (RV) 'Paul's opponents boasted of what was outward and incidental, personal knowledge of Jesus, connexion with the older apostles, Jewish descent and privilege, learning, eloquence, etc. By "heart" is meant the inward as contrasted with the outward, the essential as opposed to the incidental; so "spiritual reality." ' (Massie) [1 Sam 16:7]

*V*13: **For whether we be beside ourselves, it is to God: or whether we be sober, it is for your cause.**

For whether we have lost our wits, (it was) **for God; whether we are keeping our wits,** (it is) **for you** (Lenski) Like his Master before him, Paul was accused of religious dementia [*Mark* 3:21; *Acts* 26:24], but his 'fanaticism' was for God! Just as the Corinthians should be the last to deny the enlightening effect upon them of his lucid ministry of the gospel. The first part of the verse does not describe a state of religious ecstasy, for though Paul was no stranger to such experiences there is no reason to believe that the Corinthians ever saw him in this condition. On the contrary, he has to inform them of these *private* spiritual experiences. [1 *Cor* 14:18; 2 *Cor* 12:1] 'For God' and 'for you' are not in opposition, 'do not exclude each other as though "for God" = for him and not for you, and "for you" = for you and not for God.' (Lenski) *All* that Paul did and does is for God *and* for you.

*V*14: **For the love of Christ constraineth us; because we thus judge, that if one died for all, then were all dead:**

For the love of Christ constraineth us; It is the love of Christ for Paul which irresistibly impels him to serve God and His people in this way. This is the secret of stability in Christian service. The surpassing love of Christ for us must be reflected in our single-minded devotion to Him. [*Gal* 2:20]

because we thus judge, '*lit.*' (as) "having judged thus;" a judgment formed at conversion, and ever since regarded as a settled truth.' (Fausset)

that one died for all, therefore all died; (RV) The inescapable meaning of this statement is that the 'all' for whom Christ died are those who also died in Him. [cf. *Rom* 6:3–11; *Eph* 2:4–7; *Col* 3:3] 'The nature of the atonement settles its extent. If it merely made salvation possible, it applied to all men. If it effectively secured salvation, it had reference only to the elect. As Dr. Warfield says, "The things we have to choose between are an atonement of high value, or an atonement of wide extension. The two cannot go together." The work of Christ can be universalized only by evaporating its substance.' (Loraine Boettner, *The Reformed Doctrine of Predestination*, pp 152–153)

*V*15: **And that he died for all, that they which live should not henceforth live unto themselves, but unto him which died for them, and rose again.**

And he died for all, that they which live should no longer live unto themselves, but unto him who for their sakes died and rose again. (RV) To die with Christ is 'to die to sin and to rise with him to the life of new obedience, to live not to ourselves but to him who died for us and rose again. The inference is inevitable that those for whom Christ died are those and those only who die to sin and live to righteousness. Now it is a plain fact that not all die to sin and live in newness of life. Hence we cannot say that all men distributively died with Christ. And neither can we say that Christ died for all men, for the simple reason that all for whom Christ died also died in Christ. If we cannot say that Christ died for all men, neither can we say that the atonement is universal – it is the death of Christ for men that specifically constitutes the atonement. The conclusion is apparent – the death of Christ in its specific character as atonement was for those and those only who are in due time the partakers of that new life of which Christ's resurrection is the pledge and pattern. This is another reminder that the death and resurrection of Christ are inseparable. Those for whom Christ died are those for whom he rose again and his heavenly saving activity is of equal extent with his once-for-all redemptive accomplishments.' (John Murray, *Redemption Accomplished and Applied*, pp 70, 71)

*V*16: **Wherefore henceforth know we no man after the flesh: yea, though we have known Christ after the flesh, yet now henceforth know we him no more.**

Wherefore we henceforth know no man after the flesh: (RV) 'Wherefore' points to one consequence of the foregoing statement (*v* 15), another is advanced by the same word in the following verse. 'After the flesh' here means '*the external* or *outward side of life*, as it appears to the eye of an unregenerate person.' (Arndt-Gingrich) What Paul is saying is that since his conversion he no longer estimates any man according to worldly standards of judgment. For that which was natural to the old mode of living is entirely unnatural to one who has been raised to new life in Christ. But because the Judaizing teachers are not thus constrained by the love of Christ, they still judge 'after the flesh' and are influencing the Corinthians to regard Paul in the same way. Paul knows this tendency must be checked, for when Christians begin to look upon others in a

fleshly way, they are 'in the greatest danger of again knowing
Christ only in a fleshly way.' (Lenski)

even though we have known Christ after the flesh, (RV)
Paul does not claim personal acquaintance with Jesus; he
disowns his former unworthy estimate of Christ as a blasphemer
whose death was merited and whose followers deserved the
same treatment. [*Acts* 26:9–12) But the judgment of Saul the
unconverted Pharisee and that of Paul the believing Apostle
are poles apart.

yet now we know him so no more. (RV) It 'is not the figure
of Jesus who once wandered through the fields of Galilee, nor
is it the historical picture of the Nazarene, which forms the
content of Paul's preaching; but it is the living Lord, who has
been exalted out of his humiliation, and who as such is now the
Lord of the Church ... Yet this does not say that Paul preached
a different Jesus than the Jesus according to the flesh. Paul
preached the same Christ, but Paul now proclaims a Jesus who
died, and rose again, and who now sits at the right hand of
God, the Father. The difference does not lie in the fact that the
one picture is historical and human, whereas the other is super-
historical and divine; but it lies in the fact that the history of
redemption had progressed, that the Christ according to the
flesh is now the Lord of the heavens.' (Herman Ridderbos,
Paul and Jesus, p. 69)

*V*17: **Therefore if any man be in Christ, he is a new
creature: old things are passed away; behold, all things
are become new.**

Wherefore if any man is in Christ, there is a new creation:
(RV margin) What Paul has experienced is also true of every
man who is in Christ. Because the Christian is in fact a new
creation – 'a reborn microcosm belonging to the eschatological

macrocosm' (P. E. Hughes) – he not only has a different standard of judgment from the man of the world, but is also the
inhabitant of a totally new world. Hence the transformation
effected by his union with Christ may not be restricted to his
subjective renewal, for it includes his transfer into a world
which has assumed a new aspect and complexion. This
interpretation is required by the formula 'in Christ,' which
Paul nowhere uses in an exclusively individual sense: Christ
'is everywhere, where the formula in question occurs, the
central dominating factor of a new order of affairs, in fact
nothing less than the originator and representative of a new
world-order.' (Vos) [*Rev* 21:4, 5]

**the old things are passed away; behold, they are become
new.** (RV) 'Old opinions, views, plans, desires, principles and
affections are passed away; new views of truth, new principles,
new apprehensions of the destiny of man, and new feelings and
purposes fill and govern the soul.' (Hodge) [*Phil* 3:7]

*V*18: **And all things are of God, who hath reconciled us
to himself by Jesus Christ, and hath given to us the
ministry of reconciliation;**

But all things are of God, (RV) All these new things come
from God. 'The new creation is no spontaneous development,
and it is not man's own work on himself; Apostles do not
claim to be the cause of it. It is wholly from God [*v5*; 1:21,
2:14, 4:6; 1 *Cor.* 8:6, 11:12; *Rom* 11:36].' (Plummer)

who reconciled us to himself through Christ, (RV)
' "Reconciliation" in the New Testament sense is not something which *we accomplish* when we lay aside our enmity to
God; it is something which *God accomplished* when in the
death of Christ He put away everything that on His side
meant estrangement, so that He might come and preach

peace ... The serious thing which makes the Gospel necessary, and the putting away of which constitutes the Gospel, is God's condemnation of the world and its sin; it is God's wrath, "revealed from heaven against all ungodliness and unrighteousness of men" [*Rom* 1:16-18]. The putting away of this is "reconciliation": the preaching of *this* reconciliation is the preaching of the Gospel.' (Denney)

and gave unto us the ministry of reconciliation; (RV) That a former persecutor of the Church of God should have been entrusted with 'the ministry of reconciliation' never ceases to amaze Paul. But it is only because God has initiated and completed this great work of reconciliation that there is such a service to perform. For unless we can preach a finished work of Christ in relation to sin, a 'reconciliation or peace which has been achieved independently of us at an infinite cost and to which we are called in a word, or ministry of reconciliation, we have no real gospel for sinful men at all.' (James Denney, *The Death of Christ*, p 86)

*V*19: **To wit, that God was in Christ, reconciling the world unto himself, not imputing their trespasses unto them; and hath committed unto us the word of reconciliation.**

that is, in Christ God was reconciling the world to himself, (RSV margin) The essence of the good news is that in Christ crucified God was reconciling the world unto Himself. The term 'world' is neither to be arbitrarily limited to the elect, nor is it to be indiscriminately extended to each and every man, but it rather points to an 'eschatological' universalism. [1] For as the whole creation was involved in the consequences of the Fall, so the cosmic restoration of all things

[1]Cf. B. B. Warfield, *The Plan of Salvation*, p 102.

is secured by Christ's cancellation of the curse of sin. (P. E. Hughes) [*Rom* 8:19–21; *Col* 1:20]

not reckoning unto them their trespasses, and having committed unto us the word of reconciliation. (RV) 'The evidence that the death of Christ has been accepted as an expiation for sin, of infinite value and efficiency, is the fact that God hath commissioned his ministers to announce to all men that God is reconciled and ready to forgive, so that who-soever will may turn unto him and live.' (Hodge)

*V*20: **Now then we are ambassadors for Christ, as though God did beseech you by us: we pray you in Christ's stead, be ye reconciled to God.**

So we are ambassadors for Christ, (RSV) As the represen-tative of his sovereign, an ambassador delivers only what he has been commissioned to say, so that those who receive his message with contempt offend the king in whose name he speaks. Yet Christ's ambassadors are not quick to take offence on His behalf, and disregarding the obduracy of those to whom they are sent, they *beseech* them to receive the proferred mercy of God. [cf. *Acts* 20:21]

God making his appeal through us. (RSV) 'The fact that "God is entreating by us" is a momentous one, and the dec-laration of it is analogous to the formula of the Hebrew Prophet, "Thus saith the Lord." ' (Plummer)

'We beseech on behalf of Christ: "Be reconciled to God!" ' (P. E. Hughes) This entreaty is not addressed to the Christians in Corinth, who are here reminded of the content of the apostle's constant appeal to the unconverted. 'The synergistic reasoning is fallacious that, since God tells men to be reconciled, men must have the ability to obey. The im-perative is passive; it does not say: 'Reconcile yourselves

[73]

to God!' 'Turn *thou* me, and I shall be turned!' *Jer* 31:18. Reconcile *thou* me, and I shall be reconciled! Every gospel imperative is full of the divine power of grace to effect what it demands. If it counted on even the least power in the sinner it would never secure the least effect. Jesus calls this the Father's drawing [*John* 6:44; 6:65; 12:32].' (Lenski)

*V*21: **For he hath made him to be sin for us, who knew no sin; that we might be made the righteousness of God in him.**

In this tremendous sentence Paul explains what he means by the words, 'not imputing their trespasses unto them.' (*v* 19) The non-imputation of sin rests on the fact that Christ was made sin on our behalf. And it is this objective *satisfaction* for sin that guarantees the reality of the reconciliation which the apostle beseeches men to receive.

Him who knew no sin (RV) 'That is, with a practical know-ledge; with an intellectual he did, else he could not have reproved it. We know no more than we practise. Christ is said to "know no sin," because he did none.' (Trapp) [*John* 8:46; *Heb* 4:15; 1 *Pet* 2:22; 1 *John* 3:5]

he made to be sin on our behalf; (RV) Only He who knew no sin was free to bear its curse for others. [*Gal* 3:13] As the consequences of sin were charged to Christ's account, He became so closely identified with it that Paul even dares to say that God made Him to be *sin*. Nevertheless this is a very different thing from saying that God made Him a sinner. For though He exhausted the curse of sin, He was never personally defiled by it. 'While He was personally the object of the Father's everlasting love and complacency, He was officially guilty in our guilt. The paternal and the governmental on the part of God may easily be distinguished and viewed apart. He never was the object of the Father's loathing or aversion, even when forsaken. He never was, what the sinner inevitably is, abhorred, or abominable; because a distinction could always be made between the only begotten Son, the righteous Servant, and the sin-bearing Substitute.' (Smeaton) [*Is* 53:4, 5]

that we might become the righteousness of God in him.
(RV) As David Brown observes, 'This settles beyond dispute "*the righteousness of God*" which we "*become* in Him." For if Christ, while personally righteous, was "made sin" – not personally, but by transference to Him of our guilt, with all its penal effects – clearly "we," while personally guilty, are "made the righteousness of God in Him" by transference of His righteousness to us. Both are equally *imputative*; in both cases the act is purely *judicial*. (See *Rom* 5:18, where the same judicial sense of "*sin*" in the sense of guilt, and of "*righteousness*" in the sense of justification, is clearly intended.)

> "Our faith *receives* a righteousness
> That makes the sinner just." '

CHAPTER SIX

*V*1: **We then, as workers together with him, beseech
you also that ye receive not the grace of God in vain.**

**And working together with him we entreat also that
ye receive not the grace of God in vain,** (ARV) In the full
consciousness that he is working together with God, Paul
also appeals to the Corinthians, who have already received the
message of reconciliation, that they do not receive this grace
of God in vain. This means that there was a danger that the
forthcoming judgment [5:10] would disclose a painful discrepancy between their practice and their profession [5:15]
(P. E. Hughes) They must see to it that they receive the grace of
God *as grace*, and not as legalism or licence, or that day will
find them barren of the righteousness which is the fruit of a
living union with Christ.

*V*2: **(For he saith, I have heard thee in a time accepted,
and in the day of salvation have I succoured thee: behold,
now is the accepted time; behold, now is the day of
salvation.)**

**For he saith, At an acceptable time I hearkened unto thee,
and in a day of salvation did I succour thee:** (RV) This
parenthetic appeal to Scripture is made to remind the Corinthians that they have the inestimable privilege of living in the

promised season of grace. [*Is* 49:8] Here Paul takes the answer that God gives to the prayer of His suffering Servant (Christ) as assuring the salvation of all those for whom He is the chosen Representative.

behold now is the 'Acceptable Time,' behold now is the 'Day of Salvation.' (Bernard) Paul's own comment on the passage consists of an urgent summons to embrace the proffered favour of God in the period appointed by God for its acceptance. He thereby lets the Corinthians know that the privilege of living in such days of gospel opportunity also lays upon them the solemn responsibility of seeing that they do not receive the grace of God in vain. (*v* 1)

*V*3: **Giving no offence in any thing, that the ministry be not blamed.**

Giving no occasion of stumbling in anything, that our ministration be not blamed; (RV) The connection is with verse 1, 'we intreat . . . giving no occasion of stumbling.' The consciousness that he is a worker together with God leads the apostle to conduct himself in a manner which is consistent with the ministry he has to exercise. 'Ministers give occasion of stumbling when by their own faults they hinder the progress of the Gospel in those who hear them. Paul claims that he is not of that company and testifies to his careful concern not to stain his apostleship with any taint of disgrace. For this is a trick of Satan – to seek for a fault in ministers which will tend to bring the Gospel into disrepute. For if he succeeds in bringing the ministry into contempt, all hope of progress is gone. Thus the man who wishes to make himself useful in Christ's service must devote all his energies to maintaining the honour of his ministry.' (Calvin)

*V*4: **But in all things approving ourselves as the ministers** of God, in much patience, in afflictions, in necessities, in distresses,

V5: **In stripes, in imprisonments, in tumults, in labours, in watchings, in fastings;**

On the contrary, in everything commending ourselves, as God's ministers should do. (Plummer) Paul is not like the false teachers who brandish wordy commendations of themselves [3:1], for his whole life is a constant validation of the message he proclaims.

in much patience, It is this quality of patient endurance which enables the apostle to triumph over trials of every kind.

in afflictions, in necessities, in distresses, The first 'triplet of trials' provides a climactic description of the pressures to which he is subjected. '*In afflictions* (crushings), many ways are open, but they are all difficult; in *necessities* (constraints), one way is open, though difficult; in *distresses* (straits), none is open.' (Bengel)

In stripes, in imprisonments, in tumults, He turns next to particular hardships inflicted upon him by other men. His ministry was punctuated by beatings which would have silenced a less determined spirit [11: 23-25], frequently interrupted by imprisonments [11:23], and often abruptly halted by mob violence [*Acts* 13:50; 14:19; 16:19; 19:29].

in labours, in watchings, in fastings; Finally, he refers to the hardships he inflicted upon himself. In the cause of Christ he willingly submitted to 'wearing toil, sleepless nights, and hungry days.' (Massie) [11:27]

V6: **By pureness, by knowledge, by longsuffering, by kindness, by the Holy Ghost, by love unfeigned,**

[78]

*V*7ab: **By the word of truth, by the power of God,**

Paul has been enabled to endure all these things in virtue of those spiritual graces that constitute the sphere or element in which his ministry moves. (Fausset)

In pureness, in knowledge, (RV) In the first pair of graces, Paul significantly couples purity of life and motive with the saving knowledge of the gospel, for both are always found together in all authentic ministry.

in longsuffering, in kindness, (RV) The injuries inflicted upon Paul by the Corinthians had given him ample opportunity to exhibit his longsuffering towards them and to repay their ingratitude with kindness. [1 *Cor* 13:4; *Col* 3:12]

in the Holy Spirit, in love unfeigned, (RV margin) The holiness, of which the Holy Spirit Himself is the author, displays itself in a love that is devoid of the least tincture of insincerity or hypocrisy. [*Rom* 12:9; 1 *Pet* 1:22]

In the word of truth, in the power of God, (RV) Paul's proclamation of the word of truth was effective because he did not rely on persuasive words of wisdom to make it so, but trusted in the power of God. [1 *Cor* 2:3ff] He who is a stranger to the subjective power of the gospel in his own life cannot fittingly communicate its objective truth to others.

*V*7c: **By the armour of righteousness on the right hand and on the left,**

*V*8ab: **By honour and dishonour, by evil report and good report:**

By the armour of righteousness on the right hand and on the left, 'The weapons by which he makes the "power of God" felt are characterized by a righteous temper, and they

[79]

smite, or ward off smiting, in a righteous cause. They are not "fleshly weapons" [10:3, 4]. Paul's instruments of attack and defence, his sword and his shield, are righteous both as to means and as to end.' (Massie) [cf. *Eph* 6:13-17]

by honour and dishonour, These opposing estimates of Paul's ministry nevertheless agree in recommending the devotion with which he prosecuted it. 'Some said "He is beside himself," and others would have plucked out their eyes for his sake, yet both these extremely opposite attitudes were produced by the very same thing – the passionate earnestness with which he served Christ in the Gospel.' (Denney)

by evil report and good report: Paul continues faithful to his calling whether slandered in his absence or flattered to his face. '*In proportion as a man has more or less of glory or good report, in the same proportion has he also more or less of either disgrace or infamy respectively.*' (Bengel)

*V*8c: **As deceivers, and yet true;**

*V*9: **As unknown, and yet well known; as dying, and, behold, we live; as chastened, and not killed;**

*V*10: **As sorrowful, yet alway rejoicing; as poor, yet making many rich; as having nothing, and yet possessing all things.**

In the first three couplets Paul has in view the dishonour which was heaped upon him by the evil report of his opponents in Corinth.

As deceivers, and yet true; In branding God's inspired apostle as a purveyor of deceit, these men declare themselves to be the true children of the father of lies, thus proving their own bondage to the arch-deceiver himself. [*John* 8:44; 2 *John* 7]

As unknown, and yet well known; Paul's credentials may indeed be called in question by men, but he is confident that he is well known to God. [2 *Tim* 2:19] 'To be unknown to the world matters nothing; it is to be known of God as His own that is all-important.' (P. E. Hughes)

as dying, and, behold, we live; He is regarded by many as the doomed champion of a lost cause, but just when men are prepared to write him off as finished, all are surprised to find that he goes on living and serving His Lord.

as chastened, and not killed; Leaving these calumnies behind, Paul devotes the remaining four couplets to a para-doxical description of his actual condition. Here he thankfully acknowledges with the Psalmist, that though he is the subject of Divine chastening (though *never* of Divine wrath), God has not given him over to death. [*Ps* 118:17, 18]

As sorrowful, yet alway rejoicing; Although constantly surrounded by every kind of grief, nothing could sever him from the source of his continual rejoicing. Thus it was from the cheerless gloom of a Roman gaol that he urged his fellow-believers in Philippi to follow his own example: 'Rejoice in the Lord alway: and again I say, Rejoice.' [*Phil* 4:4]

as poor, yet making many rich; That the apostle was not well endowed with worldly wealth was evident to all, yet it was given to him to make many rich through his preaching of 'the unsearchable riches of Christ.' [*Eph* 3:8]

as having nothing, and yet possessing all things. 'It is no loss to have nothing and no gain to have everything in the way in which the world has and has not; but to have as Christians have is to have everything, no matter how little they have according to the world's way of having.' (Lenski) [1 Cor 3:21ff]

V11: O ye Corinthians, our mouth is open unto you, our heart is enlarged.

The emotions aroused in Paul by the complete lack of reserve with which he has spoken of his ministry here overflow in a sudden upsurge of feeling for his beloved converts at Corinth, to whom he addresses the tender appeal: 'O ye Corinthians.' [cf. Gal 3:1; Phil 4:15] Since such openness of speech only flows from great enlargement of heart, they should no longer doubt the genuineness of his love for them. 'Love, like heat, expands.' (Fausset)

V12: Ye are not straitened in us, but ye are straitened in your own bowels.

affections. (RV) 'The scanty room was not in him, but in the seat of their own affections, and it hampered *his* free admission to *their* hearts. Even now the feeling in Corinth towards him was not all that he could desire.' (Waite)

V13: Now for a recompence in the same, (I speak as unto my children,) be ye also enlarged.

Then surely the Corinthians must see that it is only natural that their own father in the faith should expect them to widen their hearts towards him 'in the same way in exchange.' (Arndt-Gingrich)

V14: Be ye not unequally yoked together with unbelievers: for what fellowship hath righteousness with

unrighteousness? and what communion hath light with darkness?

The sudden transition from tender entreaty to stern admonition has led many to suppose that this passage [6:14-7:1] is a mis-placed fragment from another letter, and in a number of modern commentaries the text is even re-arranged in accor-dance with this unproven and indeed unprovable hypothesis! In fact there is no evidence that any copy of the Epistle ever lacked these verses. Certainly the change in tone is abrupt, but the connection is clear enough. As Plummer rightly remarks, 'It is not incredible that in the middle of his appeal for *mutual* frankness and affection, and after his declaration that the cramping constraint is all on their side, he should dart off to one main cause of that constraint, viz. their compromising attitude towards anti-Christian influences.'

Do not try to be heterogeneously yoked up with unbe-lievers! (Lenski) The allusion is to the law which forbade the uniting of animals of different species in the same yoke. [*Deut* 22:10] 'What a picture: a believer with his neck under the unbeliever's yoke! What business has he in such an un-natural, self-contradictory association? What is he, the believer, doing by helping to pull the plough or the wagon of the unbeliever's unbelief? That yoke breaks the necks of those who bear it. God has delivered us from it; can we possibly think of going back to that frightful yoke?' (Lenski) [contrast *Matt* 11:28-30] Paul follows this command with five rhetorical questions that highlight the absolute incompatibility which exists between Christians and pagans.

For what partnership has righteousness with lawlessness? (Plummer) While it is true that in this world there are many points of contact between saints and sinners [1 *Cor* 5:10], it is self-evident that the opposing principles which characterize each class rule out any possibility of a partnership between them. For what fellowship has the *righteousness* of those who are distinguished by their habitual conformity to the law of God, with the *lawlessness* of those who are marked out by their unvarying opposition to it? [1 *John* 3:4, 9, 10]

or what communion hath light with darkness? (RV) Since nothing can be more incongruous than light and darkness, the attempt of Christians to retain their inward state as such, 'and yet to enter voluntarily into intimate fellowship with the world, is as impossible as to combine light and darkness, holiness and sin, happiness and misery.' (Hodge)

*V*15: **And what concord hath Christ with Belial? or what part hath he that believeth with an infidel?**

And what concord hath Christ with Beliar? (RV margin) This question brings into view the personal rulers behind these qualities and powers. Only the most fundamental antagonism can exist between Christ, who is the personification of righteousness, and Beliar (Satan), who is the personification of lawlessness. 'Christ hath no fellowship with the devil, therefore we ought to have no unnecessary communion with such who manifest themselves to be of their father the devil, by doing his works.' (Poole)

or what portion hath a believer with an unbeliever? (RV) 'As subjects of their respective lords, what "portion" have they together? What the one has, the other has not: righteousness, pardon, spiritual light and life, peace, hope of salvation, a place in heaven. The portions of these two diverge at every point.' (Lenski) Obviously, there can be no fellowship between those whose respective destinies are so different. But the antithesis 'must not be interpreted as though it encouraged pharisaic concepts of contamination or invited to eremitic and monastic attempts at segregation from "the world".' (P. E. Hughes)

*V*16a: **And what agreement hath the temple of God with idols?**

The climax is reached in the final question, which exhibits the utter sinfulness of attempting to find a place for the images of false gods within the imageless sanctuary of God. 'By the introduction of idols the temple ceases to be a temple of God.' (Plummer)

*V*16b: **For ye are the temple of the living God; as God hath said, I will dwell in them, and walk in them; and I will be their God, and they shall be my people.**

For we are the temple of the living God; as God said, (RSV) In boldly identifying the temple of the living God with the New Testament Church ('we' = believers), Paul here condemns the carnal expectations which are fostered by a literalistic interpretation of Old Testament prophecy. 'There cannot be a surer canon of interpretation, than that *everything which affects the constitution and destiny of the New Testament Church has its clearest determination in New Testament Scripture.* This canon, with the grounds on which it is based, strikes at the root of many false conclusions drawn mainly from ancient prophecy, respecting the events of the latter days – conclusions which always implicitly, and sometimes even avowedly, give to the Old the ascendency over the New; and, on the principle which has its grand embodiment in Popery, would send the world back to the age of comparative darkness and imperfection for the type of its normal and perfected condition.' (Patrick Fairbairn, *The Interpretation of Prophecy*, p. 158) [cf. *Eph* 2:21; 1 *Pet* 2:5]

CHAPTER 6 VERSES 17–18

I will dwell in them, and walk in them; and I will be their God, and they shall be my people. The distinctive thought of Lev 26:11-12 is that God will dwell *among* His people by means of the material sanctuary, whereas Paul's paraphrase is designed to bring out the fact that under the New Covenant He now dwells *in* them. 'Paul assumes that the ancient promise, fulfilled in outward and symbolic form in the ritual of the Tabernacle, is valid now; and assures believers of the inward and spiritual presence of God in themselves. For the entire ritual was an outward symbol of the spiritual realities of the better covenant.' (Beet) [*Ezek* 37:27]

*V*17: **Wherefore come out from among them, and be ye separate, saith the Lord, and touch not the unclean thing; and I will receive you.**

Wherefore The truth expressed in the foregoing quotation is also applied in words which are freely drawn from Scripture.

Come ye out from among them, and be ye separate, saith the Lord, And touch no unclean thing; (RV) God's warning to the returning exiles to leave everything that was unclean behind them in Babylon is here appropriately repeated to those so lately delivered from the idolatry of Corinth. [*Is* 52: 11]

and I will receive you. Such a separation is the necessary preparation for fellowship with God. [*Ezek* 20:34] 'The Christian life is thus seen to be no barren renunciation, for the believer is separated from the world for no less a purpose than that he may enjoy friendship with God in the blessed company of other faithful people.' (Tasker)

*V*18: **And I will be a Father unto you, and ye shall be my sons and daughters, saith the Lord Almighty.**

And I will be to you a Father, and you shall be to me sons and daughters, (Lenski) 'It is no common honour for us to be reckoned among the sons of God and it is for us, on our side, to take care that we do not become His degenerate children. For what an affront it is to God for us to call Him our Father and then defile ourselves with the abominations of idolatry. The thought of the great nobility He has conferred upon us ought to whet our desire for holiness and purity.' (Calvin) [2 *Sam* 7:14 with *Is* 43:6)

saith the Lord Almighty. 'The greatness of the Promiser enhances the greatness of the promises.' (Fausset)

Ch. 7 V1 : Having therefore these promises, dearly beloved, let us cleanse ourselves from all filthiness of the flesh and spirit, perfecting holiness in the fear of God.

Having therefore these promises, The word 'these' is emphatic. Paul underlines the privileges to enforce the obligations of obedience.

beloved, (RV) An intensity of meaning is given to the word by Paul's sparing use of it. [cf. 12:19; *Rom* 12:19; 1 *Cor.* 10:14; 15:58; *Phil* 2: 12; 4:1]

let us cleanse ourselves from all defilement of flesh and spirit, (RV) It is not from any sense of mock humility that Paul includes himself in this exhortation, for even an apostle must strive to attain the goal of perfection. [*Phil* 3:12–14) The determinative decisive act of cleansing is to be realized in the continual and continuing bringing of holiness to completion. Thus all believers are required by God to cleanse themselves from everything that would defile either body ('flesh') or soul ('spirit'). But those who are unwilling to cleanse themselves from every *stain* of sin only show that they have not been cleansed from the *guilt* of sin. The unsanctified are the un-justified.

perfecting holiness *Perfecting* holiness, not *perfected* holiness!

'The durative participle excludes sanctification that is attained by one act; moreover, *our* actions are here stated and not an action by which God totally sanctifies us in one instant.' (Lenski)

in the fear of God. 'This is the motive which is to determine our endeavours to purify ourselves. It is not regard to the good of others, nor our own happiness, but reverence for God. We are to be holy, because he is holy.' (Hodge) [1 *Pet* 1:14–17]

CHAPTER SEVEN

*V*1: See the end of the previous chapter.

*V*2: **Receive us; we have wronged no man, we have corrupted no man, we have defrauded no man.**

Do make a place for us in your hearts! (NEB) Here Paul resumes the appeal of ch. 6:11-13. Since the Corinthians occupy so large a place in his affections, surely they can return his love by making room for him in their hearts!

We have wronged no one, ruined no one, taken advantage of no one. (NEB) That he had harmed no one was made manifest in their consciences [5:11], and therefore he contents himself with a flat denial of the hollow charges which had been brought against him. 'Modestly he leaves them to supply the *positive* good which he had done; suffering all things himself that they might be benefited [*vv* 9, 12; 12:13].' (Fausset)

*V*3: **I speak not this to condemn you: for I have said before, that ye are in our hearts to die and live with you.**

I do not say this by way of condemnation; for I have said before that ye are in our hearts to die together and to live together. (Bernard) In thus protesting his innocence, Paul has no desire to condemn those whom he loves so completely that not even the final crisis of death, much less the vicissitudes of life, can ever erase their image from his heart. [cf. 3:2; 6:11]

V4: **Great is my boldness of speech toward you, great is my glorying of you: I am filled with comfort, I am exceedingly joyful in all our tribulation.**

Great is my confidence respecting you; great is my glorying on your behalf: (Plummer) So far from wishing to condemn the Corinthians, Paul has every confidence in them and glories greatly on their behalf.

I am filled with the comfort, I am overflowing with the joy amid all my affliction. (Plummer) 'The passives imply that someone has so filled Paul and made him overflow. The Corinthians have done this, Titus has just brought a report regarding them. The articles "with *the* consolation, *the* joy" = the one you well know as caused by you.' (Lenski)

V5: **For, when we were come into Macedonia, our flesh had no rest, but we were troubled on every side; without were fightings, within were fears.**

For even when we were come into Macedonia, our flesh had no relief, (RV) Having concluded his great 'digression' on the glory of the ministry entrusted to him by God, Paul now returns to the point at which he broke off the account of his movements in ch. 2:13. There, he says, 'I had no relief for my *spirit*'; here, 'our *flesh* had no relief.' This virtually synonymous usage shows that Paul's intense anxiety of spirit as he awaited the coming of Titus also affected his flesh, for the body is the vehicle through which the experience of the spirit finds its expression. [cf. P. E. Hughes]

but we were afflicted on every side; without were

fightings, within were fears. (RV) The situation is sketched with only three bold strokes, for Paul has no wish to dwell upon past sorrows now. Nevertheless, it is enough to let the Corinthians see something of the severity of his sufferings. For he was not only besieged by those outward troubles which were the usual accompaniment to his ministry, but he was also gripped by inward fears concerning 'the effects of his letter and of the mission of Titus.' (Massie)

*V*6: **Nevertheless God, that comforteth those that are cast down, comforted us by the coming of Titus;**

He who is 'the God of all comfort' (1:3) comforted His much tried servant by the arrival of Titus with the good news from Corinth. [cf. *Is* 49:13b] 'From this we may gather the most profitable lesson that the more we are afflicted, the greater is the comfort that God has prepared for us. And so this description of God contains a wonderful promise that it is specially God's concern to comfort the miserable and those bowed down to the dust.' (Calvin)

*V*7: **And not by his coming only, but by the consolation wherewith he was comforted in you, when he told us your earnest desire, your mourning, your fervent mind toward me; so that I rejoiced the more.**

In this verse there is a certain emphasis on the word 'your' which suggests a contrast. 'Before Titus went to Corinth, it was Paul who had been anxious to see *them*, who had mourned over their immoral laxity, who had been passionately interested in vindicating the character of the church he had founded; now it is *they* who are full of longing to see *him*, of grief, and of moral earnestness; and it is this which explains his joy. The conflict between the powers of good in one great and passionate soul, and the powers of evil in a lax and fickle community, has ended in favour of the good; Paul's vehemence has prevailed against Corinthian indifference, and made it vehement also in all good affections, and he rejoices now in the joy of his Lord.' (Denney)

V8: **For though I made you sorry with a letter, I do not repent, though I did repent: for I perceive that the same epistle hath made you sorry, though it were but for a season.**

V9: **Now I rejoice, not that ye were made sorry, but that ye sorrowed to repentance: for ye were made sorry after a godly manner, that ye might receive damage by us in nothing.**

For though I made you sorry with my epistle, I do not regret it: (ARV) 'The letter is, on the simplest hypothesis, the First Epistle; and though no one would willingly speak to friends as Paul in some parts of that Epistle speaks to the Corinthians, he cannot pretend that he wishes it unwritten.' (Denney)

though I did regret it (ARV) But after sending so stern a letter, Paul was filled with misgivings as he wondered how the Corinthians would receive it. 'Paul's admission may serve as a great comfort to us. Neither revelation nor inspiration lifted the apostles above their poor "flesh" or human nature (here mentioned twice: 7:1, 5) which asserted itself in hours of weakness and depression in the form of even doubts and regrets.' (Lenski)

(for I see that that epistle made you sorry, though but for a season), (ARV) 'Gr. for an hour. In sin, the pleasure passeth, the sorrow remaineth; but in repentance, the sorrow passeth, the pleasure abideth for ever. God soon poureth the oil of gladness into broken hearts.' (Trapp)

I now rejoice, not that ye were made sorry, (ARV) 'So careful is Paul to show that his readers' sorrow was not a matter of indifference to him. Not the immediate result, only the final result, of his letter gave joy to Paul.' (Beet)

but that ye were made sorry unto repentence; (ARV) Paul's regret (METAMELOMAI) gave way to rejoicing when he learned that their sorrow had led to their repentance (METANOIA). These words differ etymologically in that the former 'lays stress on the affliction or pain that is experienced on the contemplation of our former folly'; while the latter 'points primarily to the change of mind, issuing in amendment, which afterthought brings to us.' ('New Testament Terms Descriptive of the Great Change': *Selected Shorter Writings of Benjamin B. Warfield*, Vol. I, p 267)

for ye were made sorry after a godly sort, (ARV) When they saw their sin in the light of God's Word, they were made sorry 'in a manner agreeable to the mind and will of God; so that God approved of their sorrow. He saw that it arose from right views of their past conduct.' (Hodge)

that ye might suffer loss by us in nothing. (ARV) 'The grief of repentance is never loss in any way; not to experience this grief, that is loss indeed.' (Lenski) [cf. 'the sorrow of the world,' *v*.10]

*V*10: **For godly sorrow worketh repentance to salvation not to be repented of: but the sorrow of the world worketh death.**

For godly sorrow worketh repentance unto salvation, a repentance which bringeth no regret: (RV) Here Paul carries over the idea of regretting and not-regretting from v.8. (Lenski) Such godly sorrow, a right regret for sin, is the essential preliminary so an 'unregrettable repentance,' that gracious change of mind which always leads to salvation. Thus METANOIA (repentance) 'does not properly signify the sorrow for having done amiss, but something that is nobler than it, but brought in at the gate of sorrow.' (Jeremy Taylor, *On the Doctrine and Practice of Repentance*, cited by Trench)

but the sorrow of the world worketh death. Those who mourn over their sin turn from it and are saved; those who merely experience remorse over the bitter fruit of sin give way to despair and are lost [eg Judas Iscariot, *Matt* 27:3; Esau, *Heb* 12:17).

*V*11: **For behold this selfsame thing, that ye sorrowed after a godly sort, what carefulness it wrought in you, yea, what clearing of yourselves, yea, what indignation, yea, what fear, yea, what vehement desire, yea, what zeal, yea, what revenge! In all things ye have approved yourselves to be clear in this matter.**

For behold, this selfsame thing, that ye were made sorry after a godly sort, (RV) Behold this blessed result and admire what was wrought in you by the grace of God, for you are yourselves an example of the right kind of sorrow and its fruits!

what earnest care it wrought in you, yea, what clearing of yourselves, yea, what indignation, yea what fear, yea, what longing, yea, what zeal, yea, what avenging! (RV) 'We trace the path of sorrow working repentance here, step by step. Were they indifferent to foul sin in their midst? As repentance began in them, they became first earnestly attentive to it; then full of excuses for themselves for having neglected it; then rather indignant at the sin; then full of fear for their condoning of it; then burning with eagerness to do right; and then the repentance was fulfilled in the actual infliction of the punishment on the guilty party. The roots of it were planted in godly sorrow, its issue was amendment of life, its essence consisted in a total change of mind and heart toward their sin.' (Warfield, *op. cit.*, pp 269–270)

In everything ye approved yourselves to be pure in the matter. (RV) 'The matter' vaguely refers to what is best forgotten now that the church, through the action taken by the majority of its members, had shown itself to be free of blame in connection with the sin, which at first it appeared to condone [I *Cor* 5:2, 6].

*V*12: **Wherefore, though I wrote unto you, I did it not for his cause that had done the wrong, nor for his cause that suffered wrong, but that our care for you in the sight of God might appear unto you.**

So although I wrote unto you, I wrote not for his cause that did the wrong, nor for his cause that suffered the wrong, (RV) Clearly, Paul does not mean that he had no concern for the man guilty of incest or his outraged father, but that this was not the primary purpose in writing to them. Here Paul exhibits a common Hebrew mode of thought, in which one of two alternatives is negatived 'without meaning that it is negatived absolutely, but only in comparison with the other alternative, which is much more important. "I will have mercy, and not sacrifice" [*Hos* 6:6] does not prohibit sacrifice; it affirms that mercy is much the better of the two. [cf. *Mark* 9:37; *Luke* 10:20, 14:12, 23:28]'. (Plummer)

but that your earnest care for us might be made manifest unto you in the sight of God. (RV) By putting to the proof their full obedience, Paul aroused their dormant love and loyalty so that in the presence of God they might become aware of how much he meant to them. The issue was not at all a question of personal pique on his part; it involved nothing less than their own future as Christians. For how could they continue in fellowship with Christ while they deliberately remained in a state of alienation from His chosen apostle? (P. E. Hughes)

*V*13: **Therefore we were comforted in your comfort: yea, and exceedingly the more joyed we for the joy of Titus, because his spirit was refreshed by you all.**

Therefore we have been comforted: (RV) The perfect tense indicates that Paul has been and is comforted by the report Titus brought back from Corinth. [cf. *v*:6]

and in our comfort we joyed the more exceedingly for the joy of Titus, because his spirit hath been refreshed by you all. (RV) Moreover, Paul's joy was augmented by the joyfulness of Titus at the success of a mission that was fraught with the greatest difficulties. But the Corinthians' warm welcome and ready obedience had brought a refreshment to his spirit that was still with him (perfect tense again).

*V*14: **For if I have boasted anything to him of you, I am not ashamed; but as we spake all things to you in truth, even so our boasting, which I made before Titus, is found a truth.**

For if in anything I have gloried to him on your behalf, I was not put to shame; (RV) Although Paul did not minimize the gravity of the crisis, he believed that at heart the Corinthians were loyal and true, and he had assured Titus that his mission would be crowned with success. Happily, Paul's confidence in them was justified by the event and so he was not put to shame. This negative has the affirmative meaning: 'Your response more than verified my words to Titus.' (Lenski)

but as we spake all things to you in truth, so our glorying
also, which I made before Titus, was found to be truth.
' "My words *about* you have proved as true as my words *to*
you." A delicate hint that they should not have so readily
accepted accusations against his genuineness [1:12-14] when
he was all the while expressing confidence in them.' (Massie)

*V*15: **And his inward affection is more abundant toward
you, whilst he remembereth the obedience of you all,
how with fear and trembling ye received him.**

Titus' affection for the Corinthians is intensified as he recalls
their willingness to obey the demands he had to make, and their
'nervous and trembling anxiety to do right.' (Lightfoot on
Phil 2:12) 'This passage teaches how ministers of Christ should
be rightly received. It is not sumptuous banquets or splendid
apparel or courteous and honourable salutations or the applause
of crowds that give pleasure to a faithful and upright pastor: he
has his sufficient joy when the doctrine of salvation is reverently
received from his lips, when he can exercise the authority that
belongs to him for the upbuilding of the Church, when the
people submit themselves to his direction so as to be ruled by
Christ through his ministry.' (Calvin)

*V*16: **I rejoice therefore that I have confidence in you in all
things.**

'This expression of generous confidence is both a natural
conclusion to the present subject and a preparation for the frank
exhortation on money matters in ch. 8. It was only after the
return to mutual confidence that such matters could be
approached.' (Massie)

CHAPTER EIGHT

*V*1: **Moreover, brethren, we do you to wit of the grace of God bestowed on the churches of Macedonia;**

Now I proceed to make known to you, brethren, (Plummer) This serves to introduce a topic that deserves their close attention. [cf. 1 *Cor.* 12:3; 15:1; *Gal* 1:11] It concerns 'the collection' [1 *Cor.* 16:1], a collection 'which was not so much for "the *poor* in Jerusalem" as for "the poor in *Jerusalem*".' (K. L. Schmidt quoted by P. E. Hughes) For it was by this means that Paul hoped to give practical expression to that spiritual unity which both Jew and Gentile now enjoyed in Christ. [*Eph* 1:12–18]

the grace of God which hath been given in the churches of Macedonia; (RV) That Paul is able to devote two chapters of this Epistle to the subject of Christain giving without even mentioning the word 'money' is not only something of a *tour de force*, but it also serves to ennoble that which even Christians are apt to consider in a very materialistic manner. (Denney) Here, for example, he cites the generosity of the Macedonian churches (i.e. Philippi, Thessalonica, and presumably Berœa) as an evidence of the grace of God which is still at work in their midst.

'Thus, while holding up human excellence as an example, he shuts out beforehand all human merit.' (Beet) [*Eph* 2:10]

V2: **How that in a great trial of affliction the abundance of their joy and their deep poverty abounded unto the riches of their liberality.**

(namely) **that in a great test of affliction the excess of their joy and their down-to-depth poverty exceeded in the riches of their single-mindedness.** (Lenski) Macedonia had been reduced to a state of grinding poverty by the crippling taxes of Rome, and in the case of these Christian communities this condition was exacerbated by persecution. And though affliction filled them with abounding joy, it reduced them to such dire straits that bounty seemed impossible.' Yet these two opposites working in combination like an alkali and an acid, brought about an overflowing result which is called "the riches of their single-mindedness." Single-mindedness is that state of heart in which a man does not regard his own slender means nor any selfish consideration, but has his eye fixed exclusively upon his brother's needs. The Apostle says not that the contribution, but that the single-mindedness was rich, because it was *this* that he wished to awaken in the Corinthians. Should it operate upon Corinthian wealth instead of Macedonian poverty, the harvest would be plentiful.' (Waite)

V3: **For to their power, I bear record, yea, and beyond their power they were willing of themselves;**

V4: **Praying us with much intreaty that we would receive the gift, and take upon us the fellowship of the ministering to the saints.**

V5: **And this they did, not as we hoped, but first gave their own selves to the Lord, and unto us by the will of God.**

For in accordance with their ability, I testify, indeed,

contrary to their ability, of their own accord, with much entreaty beseeching of us the favour, namely, fellowship in the ministry to the saints, and not just as we had expected, but they gave their own selves first to the Lord and to us by the will of God. (P. E. Hughes) The verb 'gave' governs the whole of this elaborate statement, which furnishes further particulars of the liberality of the Macedonians.

1. Their help was on a scale quite beyond their slender resources. 'Despite their deep poverty they insisted on giving far more than anyone could even think they could give. They made a joy of robbing themselves.' (Lenski)

2. It was rendered so willingly that they pleaded for the privilege of being able to share in ministering to the saints. 'They begged the apostle to help them to an opportunity of acting upon the generous desire which God had implanted within them, and so of enjoying the sense of fellowship which "giving and receiving" [*Phil* 4:15] created.' (Massie)

3. Their unreserved commitment to the Lord and His apostle went far beyond Paul's expectation. Theirs was no slight contribution, for their gift was not one of money merely, 'but of themselves, first and foremost, to the Lord, who gave Himself for them [*Gal* 1:4; 2:20], and also to the apostle, as the minister, through whom Christ's self-sacrifice had been made known to them, and through whom the work of love for the saints was proceeding.' (Waite)

*V*6: **Insomuch that we desired Titus, that as he had begun, so he would also finish in you the same grace also.**

As Plummer observes, 'We are still under the influence of the rather hard-worked "gave" (*v* 5), which *sustains the whole structure of the paragraph* (Bengel).'

Accordingly we have urged Titus that as he had already made a beginning, he should also complete among you

this gracious work. (RSV) From this it appears that Titus began the task of organizing the collection in Corinth on a former visit, probably before I Corinthians was written. Dr. P. E. Hughes suggests that he also may have been the bearer of the 'lost' letter mentioned in I *Cor* 5:9. Happily, uncertainty on this point does not affect the general sense of the verse, which is well summarized by Fausset: 'As we saw the Macedonians' alacrity in giving, we could not but exhort Titus that, as we collected in Macedonia, so he in Corinth should complete the collection which he had already begun there, lest ye of wealthy Corinth should be outdone in liberality by the poor Macedonians.'

*V*7: **Therefore, as ye abound in every thing, in faith, and utterance, and knowledge, and in all diligence, and in your love to us, see that ye abound in this grace also.**

Now as you excel in everything – in faith, in utterance, in knowledge, in all earnestness, and in your love for us – see that you excel in this gracious work also. (RSV) As Paul rejoiced that in everything the Corinthians were enriched in Christ [I *Cor.* 1:5], so he desires that they also might abound in the grace of giving. For if they failed 'in this respect, it would falsify his boast that they abound *in everything*. A gentler and more urbane method of incitement to generosity it would be difficult to imagine!' (P. E. Hughes)

*V*8: **I speak not by commandment, but by occasion of the forwardness of others, and to prove the sincerity of your love.**

I speak not by way of commandment, but as proving through the earnestness of others, the genuineness also of your love. (Bernard) Because true liberality is the spontaneous expression of love, Paul refuses to command their

charity. Instead he seeks to prove the genuineness of their love
by means of the zeal of those in Macedonia. For as Hodge
pertinently remarks, 'The real test of the genuineness of any
inward affection is not so much the character of the feeling
as it reveals itself in our consciousness, as the course of action
to which it leads. Many persons, if they judged themselves by
their feelings, would regard themselves as truly compassionate; but a judgment founded on their acts would lead to the
opposite conclusion.'

*V*9: **For ye know the grace of our Lord Jesus Christ, that,
though he was rich, yet for your sakes he became poor,
that ye through his poverty might be rich.**

For ye know There is no need to command the Corinthians,
for they *know* the grand motive to Christian charity. Paul
expects their participation in this gracious work as the natural
consequence of their experimental knowledge of the grace
of Christ.

the grace of our Lord Jesus Christ, The glory of the Giver
exhibits the greatness of the grace. It is the grace which comes
to them through the infinite condescension of Him who is the
Lord to whom they owe unqualified obedience, the *Saviour*
to whom they owe their salvation, and the *Mediator* through
whom they are reconciled to God.

that, though he was rich, 'i.e. though He shared His Father's
glory before the world was created [see *John* 17:5], nevertheless He temporarily laid aside this glory in order to "be found
in fashion as a man." He did not lay aside His divinity; for
there is no doctrine of *kenōsis*, or emptying of His Godhead,
to be found here any more than in *Phil* 2:7.' (Tasker)

yet for your sakes 'Believers are to consider that Christ
impoverished Himself *for them* in order that they might be

[102]

enriched in an immeasurably higher sense than that of worldly riches and, in gratitude, they are to follow His example on a humbler level, by doing an incomparably slighter thing, sacrificing a portion of their worldly substance to supply the natural needs of those who are Christ's.' (Waite)

he became poor, The moment when 'He *became* poor' is marked by the aorist tense. It has been thought that this self-impoverishment carries an allusion to the poverty of the Lord's earthly life [*Matt* 8:20]; 'but the *primary* reference cannot be to this, for the "poverty" of Jesus Christ *by* which we are "made rich" is not the mere hardship and penury of His outward lot, but the state which He assumed in becoming man.' (Bernard)

that ye through his poverty might become rich. (RV) 'Rich in "redemption through His blood, the forgiveness of sins," rich in "peace with God through our Lord Jesus Christ," rich in "newness of life," in objects to live for and motives to live by; rich in mastery over ourselves, the world, and the wicked one, in joy unspeakable and full of glory: "all things are ours, and we are Christ's, and Christ is God's" [1 *Cor* 3:22, 23].' (Brown)

*V*10: **And herein I give my advice: for this is expedient for you, who have begun before, not only to do, but also to be forward a year ago.**

And herewith I give my opinion; what I ask is for your advantage, since you took the lead in the matter as far back as last year not only in the doing but even in the willing. (Menzies) If Paul does not command (*v* 8), he leaves the Corinthians in no doubt of his opinion on the matter. For they had anticipated the Macedonians not only in resolving to make a collection, but also in their eagerness to contribute to it. 'Having thus been beforehand with them it would be to your disadvantage to leave your work half done, seeing that the mere mention of your purpose, ch 9:2, roused them to such self-denying liberality.' (Hodge)

*V*11: **Now therefore perform the doing of it; that as there was a readiness to will, so there may be a performance also out of that which ye have.**

But now complete the doing also, that as there was the readiness to will, so there may be also the completion in accordance with your ability: (Bernard) The Corinthians' initial enthusiasm for the collection must be matched by their determination to bring it to completion. For it would be a sad thing if 'those who were foremost in willing should be hindermost in performing; they must bring their performance into line with their willingness.' (Plummer) Paul does not suggest that they should follow the example of the Macedonians by giving beyond their ability (*v* 3), but he looks for a contribution according to the measure of their ability. [cf. 1 *Cor* 16:2]

*V*12: **For if there be first a willing mind, it is accepted according to that a man hath, and not according to that he hath not.**

For if the readiness is there, it is acceptable according as a man hath, not according as he hath not. (RV) God measures the acceptability of the gift in the light of what a man has and the readiness with which it is given. 'For willingness to give is not judged by what you do not have, or, in other words, God never requires that you should contribute more than your resources allow. In this way none is left with any excuse since rich men owe God a large tribute and poor men have no reason to be ashamed if what they give is small.' (Calvin) [cf. *Mark* 12 : 41ff]

V13: **For I mean not that other men be eased, and ye burdened:**

V14: **But by an equality, that now at this time your abundance may be a supply for their want, that their abundance also may be a supply for your want: that there may be equality:**

It is not Paul's object to enrich others by impoverishing the Corinthians. He seeks an equality whereby their present wealth may supply the want of the saints in Jerusalem. Should this situation be reversed at some future date, then it would be for Jerusalem to send relief to them. He is not advocating an equality of goods, but speaks of an equal relief from the burden of want. The Scriptures 'avoid, on the one hand, the injustice and destructive evils of agrarian communism, by recognizing the right of property and making all almsgiving optional; and on the other, the heartless disregard of the poor by inculcating the universal brotherhood of believers, and the consequent duty of each to contribute of his abundance to relieve the necessities of the poor. At the same time they inculcate on the poor the duty of self-support to the extent of their ability.' (Hodge) [2 *Thess* 3:10]

V15: **As it is written, He that had gathered much had nothing over; and he that had gathered little had no lack.**

Paul finds an illustration of the principle of equality in Exodus 16:18. 'As God gave equal manna to all the Israelites, whether they could gather much or little, so Christians should promote by liberality an equality, so that none should need necessaries whilst others have superfluities.' (Fausset)

V16: **But thanks be to God, which put the same earnest care into the heart of Titus for you.**

But thanks be to God who is perpetually putting the same earnest care on your behalf in the heart of Titus. (Plummer) As Titus is to lead the delegation entrusted with the responsibility of collecting the Corinthians' gift for the saints in Jerusalem, Paul thanks God for constantly giving Titus the same zeal for their welfare as he has himself. They should realize that this earnest care is in *their* interest, for they would only rob themselves of much spiritual enrichment if they failed to make a worthy contribution to the relief-fund.

*V*17: **For indeed he accepted the exhortation; but being more forward, of his own accord he went unto you.**

For indeed he accepted our exhortation; but being himself very earnest, he went forth unto you of his own accord. (RV) When Paul urged Titus to undertake this task, his concern for the Corinthians was such that no persuasion was necessary. He was coming to them of his own accord. 'It was important for his work in Corinth that the Corinthians should know this. It was the best recommendation which Paul could send along with Titus.' (Lenski)

went forth 'We should say, *he is going* forth; but the ancients put the *past* tense in letter-writing, as the things will have been past by the time that the correspondent receives the letter.' (Fausset)

*V*18: **And we have sent with him the brother, whose praise is in the gospel throughout all the churches;**

*V*19: **And not that only, but who was also chosen of the churches to travel with us with this grace, which is administered by us to the glory of the same Lord, and declaration of your ready mind:**

Since Paul does not name the two brethren [*vv* 18, 22] who are to accompany Titus to Corinth, the attempt to identify them is quite pointless. What he is at pains to point out is that they are both tried and trusted men who have been officially appointed to perform this service by the churches (*v* 23). Moreover, the appointment proves that Paul has no personal axe to grind in forwarding this gracious work, 'which is being ministered by us to show the Lord's glory and our own readiness.' (Lenski) He seeks neither gain nor glory for himself, for his very eagerness to advance such a work of grace serves to manifest the glory of the Lord to whom he is devoted. It seems likely that this particular brother was renowned for his preaching of the gospel, though the reference may be to service of a more general nature.

*V*20: **Avoiding this, that no man should blame us in this abundance which is administered by us:**

The collection is organized by Paul, but the money will be collected by Titus and the two messengers who have been appointed by the churches for this purpose. This precaution is necessary to avoid giving anyone an opportunity to accuse the apostle of misappropriating any part of the fund. [cf. 12:17,18] He encourages the Corinthians to give generously by letting them know that he thinks of their contribution in terms of 'this lavish gift.' (Arndt-Gingrich)

*V*21: **Providing for honest things, not only in the sight of the Lord, but also in the sight of men.**

For we are taking advance thought for things honourable not only in the Lord's sight but also in the sight of men. (Lenski) 'This gives the reason for the precaution just mentioned. It was not enough for the apostle to do right, he recognized the importance of appearing right. It is a foolish pride which leads to a disregard of public opinion. We are bound to act in such a way that not only God, who sees the heart and knows all things, may approve our conduct, but also so that men may be constrained to recognize our integrity. It is a general principle regulating his whole life which the apostle here announces.' (Hodge) [cf. *Prov* 3:4 LXX and *Rom* 12:17]

*V*22: **And we have sent with them our brother, whom we have oftentimes proved diligent in many things, but now much more diligent, upon the great confidence which he hath in you.** (AV margin)

Paul commends the second brother to the Corinthians on the double ground that his earnestness in *many* things has been proved on *many* previous occasions, and that he is now *much* more earnest 'through the *great* confidence WHICH HE HAS towards you, owing to what he heard from Titus concerning you.' (Alford) The italicized words show how in the original Paul adds force to this commendation by using the same word four times.

*V*23: **Whether any do enquire of Titus, he is my partner and fellowhelper concerning you: or our brethren be enquired of, they are the messengers of the churches, and the glory of Christ.**

As for Titus, he is my partner and fellow worker in your service; and as for our brethren, they are messengers of the churches, the glory of Christ. (RSV) 'Paul extols the three in the highest terms before he sends them off; if anybody in Corinth wishes to know what they are, he is proud to tell. Titus is his partner in the apostolic calling, and has shared his work among them; the other brethren are deputies (apostles) of Churches, a glory of Christ.' (Denney) Therefore let the

CHAPTER 8 VERSE 24

Corinthians receive these duly authorized representatives in a way which befits those whose calling and character is a credit to Christ.

*V*24: **Wherefore shew ye to them, and before the churches, the proof of your love, and of our boasting on your behalf.**

Demonstrate therefore to them the demonstration of your love and of our glorying on your behalf to the face of the Churches. (Plummer) The chapter concludes 'with an exhortation to their liberality, backed with a heap of arguments. 1. It would be an evidence of their love to God, to their afflicted brethren, and to the apostle. 2. It would be a proof of it to those messengers of the churches, and to the churches whose messengers they were. 3. It would evidence that the apostle had not, to Titus and others, boasted on their behalf in vain.' (Poole)

CHAPTER NINE

V1: **For as touching the ministering to the saints, it is superfluous for me to write to you:**

Since the word 'for' indicates a continuation of the same subject, the unfortunate chapter division should be ignored. Paul has been speaking of the need for promptness in making the collection and handing it over to the brethren he is sending on in advance, a promptness which will be a public proof of love [8:24]. 'As to the service itself, the ministering to the saints, about that he need write nothing: they have been inclined for that for some time back: it is their very inclination that leads him to send on the brethren.' (Massie) [v 3]

V2: **For I know the forwardness of your mind, for which I boast of you to them of Macedonia, that Achaia was ready a year ago; and your zeal hath provoked very many.**

for I know your readiness, about which I am always boasting on your behalf to the Macedonians. 'Achaia,' I tell them, **'has been ready since last year.' And your zeal has been a stimulus to most of them.** (Plummer) Paul's boasting concerns the readiness with which the Corinthians responded when the matter of the collection was first brought before them. They 'took it up eagerly, and were

prepared to contribute at once and actually began [8:10] to
contribute. Even the liberality of the Macedonians, for which
Paul is so thankful to God, was in great part a result of the
example thus nobly set by the Corinthians. All this proves
that it is needless for him to write to them *about the collection*.
But it does not prevent him from telling them of the liberality
of the Macedonians, that the example of those whom their
own liberal purpose had aroused might prompt them to complete at once the work they had been the first to begin. Thus
example acts and re-acts.' (Beet)

*V*3: **Yet have I sent the brethren, lest our boasting of you
should be in vain in this behalf; that, as I said, ye may be
ready:**

**But I am sending the brethren, lest the boast I have made
of you should be proved an empty one in this particular,
that you might be prepared, as I said you were.** (Menzies)
Paul is confident that his boasting on the Corinthians' behalf
will be found true in every respect [8:7], except perhaps in
this one particular. Of their readiness to will [8:11] he has no
doubt, but if this is not matched by a similar alacrity in giving
he is afraid that the preparations for the collection will be
incomplete when he arrives in Corinth with the envoys from
Macedonia. It is to avoid this embarrassment that he is sending
Titus and his colleagues in advance so that his confidence in
the Corinthians may be fully justified by the event.

*V*4: **Lest haply if they of Macedonia come with me, and
find you unprepared, we (that we say not, ye) should be
ashamed in this same confident boasting.**

**lest if some Macedonians come with me and find that
you are not ready, we be humiliated – to say nothing of
you – for being so confident.** (RSV) Paul is warning the

[111]

Corinthians that when he comes to Corinth he will probably be accompanied by some Macedonians, the representatives of those whose zeal was stimulated by his account of their own enthusiasm for the collection. Let them imagine the disgrace it would be for him, to say nothing of themselves, if this visit found them still unprepared.

V5: **Therefore I thought it necessary to exhort the brethren, that they would go before unto you, and make up beforehand your bounty, whereof ye had notice before, that the same might be ready, as a matter of bounty, and not as of covetousness.**

To avoid this disgrace Paul thought it necessary to entreat Titus and his two assistants to 'come beforehand to you and set in order beforehand your blessing, which has been promised beforehand.' (Waite) The emphatic repetition makes it impossible for the Corinthians to mistake Paul's meaning. The collection they had promised so long *before* must be completed *before* his arrival in Corinth! And since this fund is intended to minister a blessing to its recipients, let them give generously to it and not in such a manner as would betray a grudging spirit.

V6: **But this I say, He which soweth sparingly shall reap also sparingly; and he which soweth bountifully shall reap also bountifully.**

As an incentive to liberality Paul reminds the Corinthians of an unvarying principle, the complete equity of which is immediately apparent; it is that the harvest reaped will be proportionate to the seed sown. [cf. *Prov* 11:24, 25; *Gal* 6:7-10] 'They who in giving think, not how little they can give, as they would if self-enrichment were their aim, but of benefits to be conferred, will receive back on the same principle. As they to others, so God will act to them.' (Beet)

V7: Every man according as he purposeth in his heart, so let him give; not grudgingly, or of necessity: for God loveth a cheerful giver.

Each man just as he has determined in his heart, (Plummer) The omission of the verb adds force to the sentence. Each man must be entirely free to decide what he will give, for Paul has every confidence that those who have freely received, will freely give. [*Matt* 10:8] 'There must be real freedom in Christian giving, each individual making the decision in his own heart how much he ought to give. It is far from Paul's intention that a "quota scheme" or a "means test" should be imposed upon the Corinthians.' (P. E. Hughes)

not from grief or from compulsion. (Lenski) 'Each is to give what he has purposed in his heart, where he is free and true: he is not to give out of grief, mourning over what he gives and regretting he could not keep it; neither is he to give out of necessity, because his position, or the usages of his society, or the comments of his neighbours, put a practical compulsion upon him.' (Denney)

For a cheerful giver God loves. (Lenski) This is taken from the LXX of Proverbs 22:8 and gives the general sense of the Hebrew: 'He that hath a bountiful (i.e. a good) eye shall be blessed.' It is the man with a generous eye who delights to devise acts of kindness who is blessed of God. For as Trapp well says, 'One may give with his hand, and pull it back with his looks.' God therefore loves the man who gives joyfully, or with hilarity (HILARON)! Then let not 'those who give reluctantly, or from stress or circumstances, or to secure merit, imagine that mere giving is acceptable to God. Unless we feel it is an honour and a joy to give, God does not accept the offering.' (Hodge)

*V*8: **And God is able to make all grace abound toward you; that ye, always having all sufficiency in all things, may abound to every good work:**

The doctrine taught is that abounding grace brings forth abounding good works. The desire to be generous and the means of being generous come from God. So Paul reminds the Corinthians that God is able to make *all* grace abound to them in order that they 'in *all* things at *all* times having *all* sufficiency, may abound to *all* good work.' (P. E. Hughes) '*What is given to us is so given and we have it, not that we may have, but that we may do well therewith. All things in this life, even rewards, are seeds to believers for the future harvest* (Bengel). The man with a bountiful heart finds that God supplies him with something to bestow.' (Plummer)

*V*9: **(As it is written, He hath dispersed abroad; he hath given to the poor: his righteousness remaineth for ever.**

As it is written, "He scatters abroad, he gives to the poor; his benevolence endures for ever." (RSV margin) Paul cites Psalm 112:9 to prove that a generous-hearted man will never lack the means to express his generosity. 'The man who fears the Lord' and gives to the needy with open-handed beneficence will not be impoverished by his benefactions. His benevolence endures for ever because God always supplies him with the resources to continue it. Such benevolence is an evidence of righteousness and not a method of attaining it.

*V*10: **Now he that ministereth seed to the sower both minister bread for your food, and multiply your seed sown, and increase the fruits of your righteousness;)**

He who supplies seed to the sower and bread for food will supply and multiply your resources and increase

the harvest of your benevolence. (RSV margin) The bountiful God who gives 'seed to the sower and bread for food'
[*Is* 55:10] will abundantly increase your resources that you
may scatter abroad acts of beneficence, as a sower scatters seed.
The final clause, which is taken from Hosea 10:12 LXX, is a
repetition of this promise, for to 'increase the fruits of your
righteousness' is to 'increase your means of doing good.'
(Hodge)

*V*11: **Being enriched in every thing to all bountifulness,
which causeth through us thanksgiving to God.**

The proximate purpose for which they are enriched with this
wealth is that 'they may exercise a single-mindedness (see on
8:2), which keeps its gaze undistracted by selfish considera-
tions and fixed solely on doing good to the poorer brethren.'
(Waite) The ultimate purpose is that those benefited by this
liberality which Paul has encouraged ('through us') will be led
to glorify God by their thanksgiving for these mercies.

*V*12: **For the administration of this service not only
supplieth the want of the saints, but is abundant also by
many thanksgivings unto God;**

**Because the ministration of this public service not only
helps to fill up the wants of the saints, but it also is abounding through many thanksgivings to God.** (Plummer)
The Corinthians are not the only contributors in this great
public service of ministering to the saints which will result in
an overflowing of many thanksgivings to God. 'Paul brings
out the distinctive feature of Christian charity. Worldly
charity is at best happy only in relieving human distress.
Pharisaic and work-righteousness charity thinks it is acquiring
merit with God. By relieving distress Christian charity delights
in the multiplied thanksgivings that will rise to God from the

hearts and the lips of those whose distress is thus relieved.'
(Lenski)

*V*13: **Whiles by the experiment of this ministration they
glorify God for your professed subjection unto the
gospel of Christ, and for your liberal distribution unto
them, and unto all men;**

**Seeing that through the proving of you by this ministra-
tion they glorify God for the obedience of your confession unto the gospel of Christ,** (RV) Moreover, the saints
at Jerusalem would see in this ministry a proof of the genuineness of the Corinthians' faith and they would glorify God
because their confession of the gospel 'finds expression in
obedient subjection to its requirements.' (Arndt-Gingrich)

**and for the single-mindedness of your fellowship with
them and with all** – (Lenski) Secondly, this tangible proof
of the reality of their confession gives evidence of their fellowship not only with the believers in Jerusalem but with all true
Christians everywhere. 'Submissive confession of the gospel
means single-minded fellowship with all the saints, all of
whom so confess and all of whom are in fellowship. The one
is never separated from the other. The one is the basis, the other
the result. Confession means fellowship, fellowship means
confession.' (Lenski)

*V*14: **And by their prayer for you, which long after you
for the exceeding grace of God in you.**

**While they themselves also, with supplications on your
behalf, long after you by reason of the exceeding grace
of God in you.** (RV) Another blessed result of this ministry
will be found in the prayers it will lead their Jewish brethren
to offer on their behalf, not only on account of the gift itself,

but also because of the exceeding grace of God which it shows is resting upon them. For it was 'a moral miracle that Macedonians and Corinthians should be exhibiting such self-sacrifice for Jews.' (Goudge) [cf. *Rom* 15:25, 26]

*V*15: **Thanks be unto God for his unspeakable gift.**

Thanks to God for his indescribable gift! (Lenski) Words fail the apostle as he contemplates the magnitude of that Gift which is beyond all human computation. There is no doubt that the indescribable gift 'for which the Apostle bursts out here into a characteristic doxology is the gift of Christ Himself [*John* 3:16] and of salvation in Him, thankful appreciation of which had borne such fruit in Christian lives.' (Bernard)

CHAPTER TEN

The marked change of tone which is so evident in ch. 10-13 has led certain critics to argue that these chapters belong to some other letter, but the Epistle is manifestly an intelligible unity as it stands. It is all about Paul's promised visit to Corinth. So if the last four chapters were not written at the same time as the first nine, 'we should not expect to find them take up the matter of the proposed visit just where it is left in ch. 9. But this is just what we do find.' (Menzies)

In this final part of the Epistle, Paul turns his attention to those who have sown the seeds of dissension in the church at Corinth. False apostles have sought to undermine his authority, and at the same time to discredit his gospel, by speaking disparagingly of his 'weakness.' It is therefore entirely natural and eminently sensible that he should answer these attacks and vindicate his apostolic authority before he visits them again. 'The Corinthians must make up their minds, *all* of them, whether Paul is really their apostle or not. There must be no longer any kind of hesitation about this. It is as their apostle by divine commission that he is going to visit them once again, claiming the allegiance that is his due.' (Tasker)

V1: **Now I Paul myself beseech you by the meekness and gentleness of Christ, who in presence am base among you, but being absent am bold toward you:**

Now I Paul myself This 'is not only the grammatical subject of the sentence, but if one may say so, the subject under consideration; it is the very person whose authority is in dispute who puts himself forward deliberately in this authoritative way.' (Denney)

beseech you by the meekness and gentleness of Christ, The apostle cannot have been as ignorant of the Lord's earthly life as some modern scholars imagine, for this appeal assumes a knowledge of the character of Christ which the Corinthians must have owed to his instruction. Paul knows that he is despised for following the example of Him whose 'meekness' of heart [*Matt* 11:29] was shown by his 'gentleness' in dealing with poor sinners [e.g. *John* 8:1–11], but he hopes that they will not put his courage to the test! (*v* 2)

I who am humble when face to face with you, but bold to you when I am away! (RSV) This is the only place in the New Testament where 'humble' (TAPEINOS) is used in a bad sense. Paul is echoing the contemptuous accusation of his proud critics who had not learned the Christian meaning of the word. (Denney) 'They had said that, when he was there, he was a Uriah Heep, very humble and cringing and artful; when he was away from them, he could pluck up his courage and be very resolute – on paper.' (Plummer)

V2: **But I beseech you, that I may not be bold when I am present with that confidence, wherewith I think to be bold against some, which think of us as if we walked according to the flesh.**

Yea, I beseech you, that I may not when present shew courage with the confidence wherewith I count to be bold against some, which count us as if we walked according to the flesh. (RV) Paul even begs the Corinthians not to force him to display when present that courage which is only attributed to him when absent. Indeed he is resolved to act with the greatest boldness against certain persons who wrongly reckon that his conduct is dictated by purely worldly motives. 'His Corinthian detractors judged him by themselves, as if he were influenced by fleshly motives, desire of favour, or fear of offending, so as not to exercise his authority.' (Fausset)

V3: **For though we walk in the flesh, we do not war after the flesh:**

In the flesh (emphatic) **no doubt we walk, but not according to the flesh do we carry on our warfare.** (Plummer) Since Paul is a man he is obliged to walk *in* the flesh, but his opponents have greatly misjudged him in thinking that he walks *according to* the flesh. They thought it would be an easy matter to destroy Paul with the carnal weapons in their armoury, but they will shortly discover to their dismay that he neither *walks* nor *wars according to* the flesh. Certainly he will fight these enemies of the gospel to the finish, but not on their terms nor with their weapons.

V4: **(For the weapons of our warfare are not carnal, but mighty through God to the pulling down of strong holds;)**

(For the weapons of our warfare are not carnal, 'In the war in which Paul was engaged, his confidence was not in himself, not in human reason, not in the power of arguments or eloquence, not in the resources of cunning or management, but simply and only in the supernatural power of God.' (Hodge) [*Zech* 4:6]

but mighty through God to the pulling down of strong holds;) The cause of Christ is never advanced by carnal methods because the strongholds in which sinners entrench themselves will never yield to the bravest display of worldly weapons. It is only before the resistless power of God, that the walls of these fortresses fall flat [*Josh* 6:20]

V5: Casting down imaginations, and every high thing that exalteth itself against the knowledge of God, and bringing into captivity every thought to the obedience of Christ;

Casting down reasonings, (AV margin) This warfare is not carnal, for the strongholds that Paul is engaged in demolishing are not the *persons* of the unbelieving, but the sinful *reasonings* – 'the refuge of lies' – by which they seek to fortify themselves against the knowledge of God. The military metaphor 'emphasizes the defiant and mutinous nature of sin: sinful man does not wish to know God; he wishes himself to be the self-sufficient centre of his universe.' (P. E. Hughes) [cf. *Rom* 1:18ff.]

and every high thing that exalteth itself against the knowledge of God, 'Such were the *high towers* of Judaic self-righteousness, philosophic speculations, and rhetorical sophistries, the "knowledge" so much prized by many, which opposed the "knowledge of God" at Corinth. True knowledge makes men humble. Where self is exalted God is not known.' (Fausset)

and bringing every thought into captivity to the obedience of Christ; Such a deliverance from the proud ramparts of 'autonomous' reason has the supremely positive purpose of bringing 'every intention of the mind' (Alford) into subjection to the *obedience of Christ* without which there can be no true *knowledge of God*. But though this is always true of the regenerate in principle, unhappily it is not always so in practice. And Paul intends the Corinthians to see that it was because they had failed fully to submit themselves to the mind of Christ that they were being deceived by the specious logic of the false apostles. (P. E. Hughes) [cf. 11:2 ff.]

*V*6: **And having in a readiness to revenge all disobedience, when your obedience is fulfilled.**

And being in readiness to avenge all disobedience, when your obedience shall be fulfilled. (RV) When Paul at last returns to Corinth those who have charged him with uttering empty threats will find to their dismay that he is more than ready to punish the disobedient. Meanwhile he 'charitably assumes that the Corinthian church will act obediently; therefore he says "YOUR obedience." But as some will act otherwise, in order to give all an opportunity of joining the obedient, he waits (not prematurely exacting punishment) until the full number of those who obey Christ has been "completed," and the remainder have proved incorrigible.' (Fausset)

*V*7: **Do ye look on things after the outward appearance? If any man trust to himself that he is Christ's, let him of himself think this again, that, as he is Christ's, even so are we Christ's.**

Look at what is before your eyes. (RSV) 'The rendering, Do you look at what is before your face? makes the sequence difficult; what the Apostle proceeds to point out is not something the Corinthians have interpreted wrongly, but something they must see to be the case when they look at it.' (Menzies)

If any one is confident that he is Christ's, let him remind himself that as he is Christ's, so are we. (RSV) This is an ironical reference to the arrogant claims advanced by his opponents. Should such a one regard himself as an apostle of

Christ to whom the church at Corinth must defer, let him also consider that Paul's claim to exercise the same authority is no less emphatic than his own. Moreover, in his case this personal conviction can be substantiated with objective credentials which cannot be matched or gainsaid by these wordy claimants to a superior apostleship. [cf. 3:2, 12:2; 1 Cor 9:2]

*V*8: **For though I should boast somewhat more of our authority, which the Lord hath given us for edification, and not for your destruction, I should not be ashamed:**

Paul knows that his critics have accused him of boasting, but even if he were to make higher claims for his ministry he is confident that he would have no cause to be ashamed of his words. He is not like those who must try to bolster up their position with empty boasting, for the reality of his claims is amply borne out by the facts. Because the Lord Himself not only appointed him to this office, but his authority as an apostle is always exercised in accordance with the terms of that Divine mandate. All his efforts are directed towards the building up of the church, whereas the false apostles used their assumed authority to destroy it. What he says here is no contradiction of verse 5. For though 'we "cast down reasonings," this is not in order to destroy, but to *build up*, by removing hindrances to edification, testing what is unsound, and putting together all that is true in the building.' (Chrysostom cited by Fausset)

*V*9: **That I may not seem as if I would terrify you by letters.**

But Paul refrains from saying anything more about his authority lest he should seem to justify the jibe of his opponents by scaring the Corinthians out of their wits with his letters! A sarcasm which effectively reveals the absurdity of the accusation.

*V*10: **For his letters, say they, are weighty and powerful; but his bodily presence is weak, and his speech contemptible.**

For, His letters, they say, are weighty and strong; (RV) It is worth noting that even Paul's detractors were forced to admit that there was nothing weak about his letters. 'The saying is a valuable testimony to the impression the Epistles of Paul at once produced when they were written; they were felt to be grave and important utterances, and they acted effectively, as they were intended to do.' (Menzies) It has not since proved necessary to revise this contemporary estimate of the power of Paul's pen.

but his bodily presence is weak, and his speech of no account. (RV) 'Paul may write, bold, bluffing letters, but when he appears in person he cannot disguise his weakness and then his speech amounts to nothing!' Misjudging Paul's motives, his enemies mistook meekness for weakness [11:21], and branded his artless preaching as being unworthy of the attention of educated Greeks! [11:6; 1 *Cor* 1:17; 2:1-5]

*V*11: **Let such an one think this, that, such as we are in word by letters when we are absent, such will we be also in deed when we are present.**

Anyone who is tempted to believe that slander should think again. Let him rather count ('reckon' RV) on the fact that Paul's forthcoming visit will prove that he lacks neither the determination nor the courage to discipline the disobedient. Then it would be evident to all that there was no discrepancy whatever between his words and his deeds. [13:2, 10]

*V*12: **For we dare not make ourselves of the number, or compare ourselves with some that commend themselves: but they measuring themselves by themselves, and comparing themselves among themselves, are not wise.**

For we are not bold to number or compare ourselves with certain of them that commend themselves: (RV) However, Paul ironically confesses that he does not have the courage to class or compare himself with certain of those 'who make self-commendation, unsupported by any corroborating evidence, their title to fame.' (Tasker)

but they themselves, measuring themselves by themselves, and comparing themselves with themselves, (RV) 'Instead of the public standard, they measure themselves by one made by themselves: they do not compare themselves with others who excel them, but with those like themselves; hence their high self-esteem. The one-eyed is easily king among the blind.' (Fausset) [cf. *Matt* 5:20]

are without understanding (RV) Their fancied wisdom is in fact arrant folly! 'These self-satisfied critics, who have no external standard, but judge everything by comparison with their own practice, come very far short of wisdom.' (Plummer)

*V*13: **But we will not boast of things without our measure, but according to the measure of the rule which God hath distributed to us, a measure to reach even unto you.**

But we will not glory beyond measure, (RV) It is not for Paul to compete with those who glory only in themselves, though it is not surprising that those who know nothing of God's standard of measurement are well satisfied to measure

[125]

themselves by themselves. These false apostles would be trespassing wherever they went, for the very 'gospel' [11:4] they preached was an indisputable proof that no sphere of labour had been marked out for them by God. But Paul's glorying is legitimate for he glories in the Lord who called him and who appointed the bounds of his service.

but according to the measure of the province which God apportioned to us as a measure, to reach even unto you. (RV) The Judaizers boasted of gifts they did not possess and battened like parasites on churches which they had not founded. Paul did not indulge in such inordinate boasting and it was his settled practice not to build on another man's foundation. [*Rom* 15:20] It was he, and not they, who had brought the gospel as far as Corinth; and since his labours there were the instrumental means of bringing the Corinthians to a living faith in Christ, they of all people ought to be the last to doubt the authority of his apostleship over them. [*1 Cor* 9:1, 2]

*V*14: **For we stretch not ourselves beyond our measure, as though we reached not unto you: for we are come as far as to you also in preaching the gospel of Christ:**

We are not overstretching our commission, as we should be if it did not extend to you, (NEB) 'The farther Paul penetrated the Gentile world with the gospel, the nearer he came to the mark and the measure which God had set for him.' (Lenski)

for we were the first to reach Corinth in preaching the gospel of Christ. (NEB) Paul's point is not merely that he was the first to reach Corinth, but that he was the first to reach it with *the gospel of Christ.* For these emissaries of Jewish legalism who had followed him there brought with them 'another

gospel which is not another.' [*Gal* 1:6, 7] 'They made it their
business to follow in Paul's tracks, to steal into his congrega-
tions, and then to undermine his gospel work. They had not
even a commission from God, to say nothing of a mark of
measurement that had been set by God, which they were to
reach. Theirs was the devil's work [11:3, 4].' (Lenski)

*V*15: **Not boasting of things without our measure, that is,
of other men's labours; but having hope, when your
faith is increased, that we shall be enlarged by you
according to our rule abundantly,**

**I do not boast beyond due measure by intruding upon a
sphere in which others have been commissioned to
labour;** (Bruce) Paul's 'enemies spoke and acted as if the
fruits of his missionary toil had been produced by them.
Against this lawless and vaulting ambition he sets his own
aspirations.' (Waite)

**I have good hope that, as your faith increases, my own
sphere of labour will be increased the more by your aid,
according to the commission which I have been given.**
(Bruce) He hopes that the Corinthians will help him to fulfil
his calling, for it is only when increased faith restores them to
full obedience that he will feel free to undertake further
responsibilities in claiming new territory for Christ.

*V*16: **To preach the gospel in the regions beyond you, and
not to boast in another man's line of things made ready
to our hand.**

so that we may preach the gospel in lands beyond you,
(RSV) Paul possibly refers to his projected visit to pagan Spain.
[*Rom* 15:24]

without boasting of work already done in another's field. (RSV) The repetition 'reveals Paul's deep sense of how unjust is his opponents' boasting. While his thoughts about the Corinthians, whom he had led to Christ, were that their increasing faith would enable him to break up new ground still further off, his opponents were exulting about things in a field allotted by God to Paul, and in reference to work which they found *already done*. With such men Paul dares not compare himself.' (Beet)

*V*17: **But he that glorieth, let him glory in the Lord.**

With this quotation of a favourite text Paul puts his own glorying in the right light, and at the same time passes censure upon his opponents. (Massie) [*Jer* 9:23, 24; 1 *Cor* 1:31] The way in which the New Testament writers freely apply or transfer to Christ references in the Old Testament to Jehovah 'is a significant pointer to the fundamental apostolic belief in the pre-existence of Christ in the unity of the eternal Godhead.' (P. E. Hughes)

*V*18: **For not he that commendeth himself is approved, but whom the Lord commendeth.**

Paul has been forced by the attacks made on him to boast about himself, but it was not on this self-praise that he relied. It was ever and only the Lord's approval that he sought, and the manifest blessing which rested upon his work at Corinth and elsewhere proved that he did not lack the tangible tokens of it. The very existence of the Corinthian Church was *his* letter of commendation. [3:2] But his 'assailants had no such confirmation of the praise which they bestowed on themselves.' (Plummer)

In the final analysis all will be constrained to admit that the

Lord's commendation is the only one that matters [1 *Cor* 4:3, 4], but those who do not seek to please Him *now* will find to their everlasting sorrow and shame that it is too late to do so *then*.

CHAPTER ELEVEN

Paul finds it distasteful to boast about himself, but the tactics of his rivals are forcing him to descend to their level. If he now assumes the fool's mask for a little while, it is because his concern for the Corinthians leads him to expose the folly that is so entirely natural to the men who had deceived them with their great swelling words. In this chapter he sweeps aside the empty boasting of these vocal pretenders to the apostolate with a devastating revelation of what it cost him to be faithful to his commission.

*V*1: **Would to God ye could bear with me a little in my folly: and indeed bear with me.**

Would that ye could bear with me in a little foolishness: but indeed ye do bear with me. (ARV) With magnificent irony Paul begins by wishing that the Corinthians would bear with him in a little of the folly of self-boasting! But he immediately corrects himself, for after all such an appeal is quite superfluous when they are so practised 'in enduring the overbearing demeanour of his opponents! [verse 20]' (Massie)

*V*2: **For I am jealous over you with godly jealousy: for I have espoused you to one husband, that I may present you as a chaste virgin to Christ.**

For I am jealous over you with God's jealousy, (Lenski) 'This is why he plays the fool,' says Calvin, 'for jealousy sweeps a man off his feet.' But the jealousy Paul feels is not for himself or his own reputation, it is a jealousy he endures on God's behalf. His feelings towards the Corinthians are in certain respects analogous to those of Jehovah over faithless Israel.

for I espoused you to one husband, (RV) Paul is the match-maker through whom a marriage has been arranged between Christ and the Corinthians, but he is beginning to be fearful for the purity of the prospective bride. 'It is necessary that the bride should concentrate her attention on the "one man" to whom she is engaged, and not open her heart to any other; but there is reason to fear that the Corinthian Church is having its attention distracted from the true object, namely, from Christ as He was preached by Paul. He is afraid that this bride is allowing other views to be introduced into her mind, views inconsistent with her first loyalty.' (Menzies)

that I might present you as a pure virgin to Christ. (RV) 'As in Eph 5:27 this presentation of the church to Christ as his bride, is said to take place at his second coming, this passage is commonly understood to refer to that event. Paul's desire was that the Corinthians should remain faithful to their vows, so as to be presented to Christ a glorious church, without spot or wrinkle, on that great day. He dreaded lest they should, in that day, be rejected and contemned as a woman unfaithful to her vows.' (Hodge)

*V*3: **But I fear, lest by any means, as the serpent beguiled Eve through his subtilty, so your minds should be corrupted from the simplicity that is in Christ.**

But I fear, lest by any means, as the serpent beguiled Eve

in his craftiness, your minds should be corrupted from the simplicity (the single-mindedness) **that is toward Christ.** (Brown) 'What Paul dreads is the spiritual seduction of the Church, the winning away of her heart from absolute loyalty to Christ. The serpent beguiled Eve by his craftiness; he took advantage of her unsuspecting innocence to wile her away from her simple belief in God and obedience to Him . . . The serpent's agents – the servants of Satan, as Paul calls them in verse 15 – are at work in Corinth; and he fears that their craftiness may seduce the Church from its first simple loyalty to Christ.' (Denney) [*Gen* 3:13]

*V*4: **For if he that cometh preacheth another Jesus, whom we have not preached, or if ye receive another spirit, which ye have not received, or another gospel, which ye have not accepted, ye might well bear with him.**

For The connection is with verse 1. When the Corinthians bear with the false apostles so well, they should not find it too difficult to put up with their genuine apostle for a little while!

if This denotes a condition of reality. Paul does not point to any imaginary danger but describes the actual situation in Corinth.

he No particular individual is in view. The actions of one false teacher are representative of all who are like him.

that cometh Of his own volition, as opposed to being commissioned and sent by God. These men 'had simply *come*, unsent and without divine authorization; and therefore they were no apostles.' (P. E. Hughes) [*v* 13]

preacheth another Jesus, whom we did not preach, (RV) Paul consigns to a decent oblivion the precise nature of his

opponents' teaching, but it is hardly likely that he would have
overlooked a defective Christology without comment. On
this assumption the contrast would not be between their
human Jesus and his heavenly Christ. It would seem a far more
reasonable surmise to suggest that in transforming the gospel
into a scheme of salvation by works, these Jewish legalists in
effect preached 'another Jesus' even though they held to an
orthodox view of His Person, including the confession of His
Deity.

**or if ye receive a different spirit, which ye did not
receive.** (RV) An ironical allusion to the powerlessness of the
Judaizers to impart the Holy Spirit. (Beet) They are dispensers
of a different spirit, a spirit which is consonant with the
doctrine taught. It is the spirit 'which gendereth to bondage.'
[cf. *Gal* 5:1, 4]

or a different gospel, which ye did not accept, (RV) It was
in connection with Paul's preaching of Jesus as the *Saviour* of
sinners that the Corinthians received the Spirit through whom
they were able to accept the *one* authentic gospel. 'The will of
man is passive in RECEIVING the "Spirit;" but it is actively
concurrent with the will of God (which goes before to give
the good will) in ACCEPTING the "Gospel".' (Fausset) But to
give heed to a man who preaches *another* Jesus is to receive a
different spirit and to accept a *different* gospel!

you put up with it well enough! (Arndt-Gingrich) A
cutting reflection on their disloyalty to him. '*He* had to plead
for their toleration, but they had no difficulty in tolerating
men who by a spurious gospel, an unspiritual conception of
Christ, and an unworthy incapacity for understanding freedom,
were undermining his work, and seducing their souls.'
(Denney)

V5: **For I suppose I was not a whit behind the very chiefest apostles.**

for I reckon that I am in nothing behind the superlative apostles! (Waite) 'What a pity you find it so easy to tolerate these superfine apostles when my credentials are in no way inferior to theirs!' Paul is not seriously comparing himself with the false apostles (*v* 13), 'but speaking with incisive bitterness of the supposed position of inferiority which they had tried to assign to him.' (Waite)

V6: **But though I be rude in speech, yet not in knowledge; but we have been throughly made manifest among you in all things.**

But though I am untrained in oratory, yet in knowledge I am not so; (Plummer) This concession to the criticism of his enemies is also tinged with irony. If Paul's speech was devoid of the ornamental flourishes of a man trained in the art of rhetoric, its content was certainly not deficient in knowledge as the Corinthians had good cause to know. [cf. 1 *Cor* 2] But it is the mark of an infantile mind to be more concerned with the wrappings than the contents of the parcel!

but in all things we made it manifest among all men to you-ward. (Plummer) In pursuance of his Divine commission to manifest the truth to every man's conscience [4:2], Paul has made known this knowledge without the slightest reserve, freely declaring the whole counsel of God to all who would listen to him.

V7: **Have I committed an offence in abasing myself that ye might be exalted, because I have preached to you the gospel of God freely?**

Or did I commit a sin in abasing myself that ye might be exalted, because I preached to you the gospel of God for nought? (RV) Or perhaps the Corinthians prefer these false gospellers because they have had to pay for the privilege of being deceived by them? Evidently Paul's opponents had said that his refusal to accept maintenance from the Corinthians was a tacit admission of his amateur status, for a proper apostle would have received it as a right! [v 12; cf. 1 Cor 9:4–19] 'Christ's pure Gospel without price and the corrupted doctrine of the Judaizers at a cost [11:20]; his self-abasement and their self-glorification; his emancipation and their enslaving of the community, are pointed contrasts.' (Waite)

V8: **I robbed other churches, taking wages of them, to do you service.**

Paul even "robbed" other churches, i.e. 'accepting support so that I might serve you.' (Arndt-Gingrich) He accepted a subsistence from other churches which were not receiving the benefits of his ministry in order that he might minister the gospel without charge to the Corinthians. Paul rubs in this truth and makes it smart 'to drive out their mean ingratitude. For what is meaner than to slander a benefactor for bestowing his benefaction *gratis*?' (Lenski)

V9: **And when I was present with you, and wanted, I was chargeable to no man: for that which was lacking to me the brethren which came from Macedonia supplied: and in all things I have kept myself from being burdensome unto you, and so will I keep myself.**

And when I was present with you and was in want, (RV) While present with the Corinthians Paul ran short of funds and found himself in want, 'his handicraft and the narrow margin of time which was all that he could devote to it not sufficing for his support.' (Waite) [*Acts* 18:3]

I was not a burden on any man; (RV) Even when without visible means of support Paul was a dead weight on no one in Corinth. KATANARKAŌ, 'to be a burden, to be burdensome, primarily signifies to be numbed or torpid, to grow stiff (*narkē* is the torpedo or cramp fish, which benumbs anyone who touches it); hence to be idle to the detriment of another person (like a useless limb).' (Vine)

for the brethren, when they came from Macedonia, supplied the measure of my want; and in everything I kept myself from being burdensome unto you, (RV) During the whole of his mission to Corinth Paul studiously avoided taking any financial assistance from the Corinthians, and he owed this independence in a large measure to the unstinted generosity of the Macedonian churches.

and so will I keep myself. And whatever the mercenary-minded Judaizers might say about it, Paul is determined to maintain this independence on his forthcoming visit.

*V*10: **As the truth of Christ is in me, no man shall stop me of this boasting in the regions of Achaia.**

Paul, conscious of the fact that he speaks in conformity with the truthfulness of Christ, here avers that 'this boasting will not (let itself) be stopped.' (Arndt-Gingrich) Despite the desperate attempts of his enemies to stop (i.e. to block by barricade or damming up) the flow of his boasting about preaching without payment, they will not succeed either in Corinth or indeed throughout all Achaia. (Lenski)

*V*11: **Wherefore? because I love you not? God knoweth.**

It would seem that the false apostles had insinuated it was because Paul cared so little for the Corinthians that he refused to take their money, whereas *they* had enough affection for them to receive it! Can they really find it in their hearts to believe that he is too proud to be indebted to those to whom he is indifferent? (Massie) If they did not know him better than that, there is One who does. God, before whom no secrets are hid, takes full cognizance of the strength of his feeling for them, and knows the real reason for his refusal to accept their support.

V12: But what I do, that I will do, that I may cut off occasion from them which desire occasion; that wherein they glory, they may be found even as we.

But what it is my practice to do that I will also continue to do, in order that I may remove the opportunity from those that desire an opportunity for being found on a level with me in the work in which they boast. (P. E. Hughes) Paul's rivals will be disappointed if they hope that their criticism of his disinterestedness will induce him to follow their lead in accepting money from the Corinthians. For he is determined not to afford them any pretext for claiming that their nefarious work of deception has even a semblance of equality with the authentic ministry which he exercises. 'Paul was too capable a strategist to surrender such a position to the enemy. It would never be by any action of his that he and they found themselves on the same ground.' (Denney)

V13: For such are false apostles, deceitful workers, transforming themselves into the apostles of Christ.

Not a few have questioned the Apostle's wisdom in using such 'intemperate' language, but as Bengel finely observes, 'the Indifferentism, which is so pleasant to many in the present day, was not cultivated by Paul. He was no pleasant preacher of

[137]

toleration.' But the truth is always intolerable to those who are distinguished by their easy toleration of every conceivable deviation from the faith once delivered to the saints. Today when every babbler of error is almost certain to be hailed as an apostle of Christ by a degenerate Christianity, it is high time for those who remain faithful to the testimony of Jesus to sound no uncertain note of warning. The moment is long overdue for professed Evangelicals to stop fêting the traducers of their Lord and to recognize these men for the deceitful workers they are.

fashioning themselves into apostles of Christ. (RV) They changed their outward appearance by assuming the guise of Christ's servants, but their essential character as the slaves of Satan remained unchanged. 'They pose as something which they are not, and in doing so they deceive those who through gullibility or inexperience are more ready to give credence to plausible imposters than to remember the sound teaching and warnings of him who is their true apostle.' (P. E. Hughes)

*V*14: **And no marvel; for Satan himself is transformed into an angel of light.**

It is no wonder that those who are in reality opposed to Christ should wish to be taken for His apostles, for in this they are merely following the practice of their true master! Satan's masquerading by deceit as a messenger of light, i.e. as the herald of true knowledge, is but the pattern of his conduct as the deceiver, from his first dealings with mankind in the Garden of Eden [cf. *v* 3]. Because it is only by posing as the champion of truth that the prince of darkness is able to persuade men to swallow his lies.

*V*15: **Therefore it is no great thing if his ministers also be transformed as the ministers of righteousness; whose end shall be according to their works.**

It is therefore no great thing, 'if Satan's power to present himself in a guise foreign to his real nature should also be found in those enlisted in his service. Appearing as *the ministers of righteousness*, i.e. eloquent advocates of the Pharisaic doctrine that men can put themselves right with God by their own unaided efforts, they are in fact deceivers of others because they are themselves deceived.' (Tasker) [cf. *Acts* 13:39; *Rom* 10:3; *Gal* 2:21; *Phil* 3:6, 9]

whose end shall be according to their works. Their end will be according to their Satanic deeds, and not according to their apostolic pretensions! [5:10] Then those who thought that they were saved by 'works' will discover to their eternal confusion that these were not sufficient to secure them a place among the redeemed.

*V*16: **I say again, Let no man think me a fool; if otherwise, yet as a fool receive me, that I may boast myself a little.**

I say again, Let no man think me foolish, (RV) Paul again makes clear his extreme reluctance to indulge in the same folly as the Judaizers. (*v* 1) He wishes the Corinthians to understand that though such boasting is natural to the false apostles, he is only acting a part which has been forced upon him by their accusations.

but even if ye do, yet receive me as foolish, that I also, may glory a little. (Bernard) But if they insist on regarding him as a fool then let them *also* listen to a little of *his* foolishness. After all, this should be no hardship to those who are so ready to welcome fools with open arms!

*V*17: **That which I speak, I speak it not after the Lord, but as it were foolishly, in this confidence of boasting.**

I speak not after the Lord To regard this as a disclaimer of either the authority or the inspiration of the Lord is not only to discount the value of Paul's utterance for the church but also to do him a grave injustice. Lenski brings out the true meaning of the verse: 'This foolish boasting will not follow the norm and principle of Jesus, for it will be done, not, indeed, "*in* folly," yet "*as in* folly." It will look like folly. It will thus stoop to a lower norm than Jesus used. If it were done in actual folly it would, of course, be stooping to sin; since it is done only in apparent folly it is not sin but is ethically on a lower plane than the one on which Jesus moved.' This explains why Paul is so reluctant to glory, but he is going to do so in order to bring the Corinthians to their senses.

*V*18: **Seeing that many glory after the flesh, I will glory also.**

After the flesh here means to 'boast of one's outward circumstances, i.e. descent, manner of life, etc. [cf. *v* 22].' (Arndt-Gingrich) Since his opponents wax eloquent in extolling their external advantages Paul will meet them on the same ground to show the Corinthians that even at this low level of boasting he is not a whit behind these superlative apostles! (*v* 5)

*V*19: **For ye suffer fools gladly, seeing ye yourselves are wise.**

fools . . . wise 'The Greek antithesis is "senseless, sensible." The irony cuts at the Corinthian self-sufficiency, which blinds them to what real folly is. "Foolish are these boasters; but you plume yourselves on your shrewdness in accepting them. So you will, I am sure, accept me when I talk like them.' (Massie)

*V*20: **For ye suffer, if a man bring you into bondage, if a man devour you, if a man take of you, if a man exalt himself, if a man smite you on the face.**

Why, you bear it if one enslaves you, if one devours (you), if one captures (you), if one lifts himself up (over you), if one smites you in the face! (Lenski) Paul knows that the Corinthians will put up with *him* when they are so patiently enduring the indignities which are being heaped upon them by these tyrannical teachers! Not only have they suffered these things, for all the 'ifs' denote reality, 'but the conditional form also implies that they are ready to have it repeated again and again.' (Lenski)

1. They were being enslaved. In forfeiting Christian liberty for the yoke of Jewish legalism, they were exchanging their spiritual freedom for abject bondage. [*Gal* 2:4; 5:1]

2. They were being exploited. 'Devours' vividly describes the rapacious exactions of the Judaizers which they justified on the grounds of apostolic rights! [cf. *Luke* 20:47]

3. They were being ensnared. This word pictures them as caught by the crafty cunning of these unscrupulous hunters of the souls of men.

4. They were being dominated. The false apostles made free use of their usurped authority to lord it over the Corinthians.

5. They were being humiliated. To crown it all, it would seem that their new masters even resorted to physical violence. This was doubtless done 'under the pretext of divine zeal. The height of insolence on their part, and of servile endurance on yours [*1 Kings* 22:24; *Neh* 13:25; *Luke* 22:64; *Acts* 23:2; *1 Tim* 3:3].' (Fausset)

*V*21a: **I speak as concerning reproach, as though we had been weak.**

To my shame, I must say, we were too weak for that! (RSV) This final shaft brings Paul's biting satire to a shattering climax. He might well have said, 'What a disgrace *for you* to have received such fellows *gladly*!' Instead he says, 'No, the disgrace is mine, for *we* were too *weak* to treat you like that!'

[cf. 10:10] Yes, these 'false apostles know how real apostles ought to act so as to impress you with what real apostles are; *we* – why, we did not even know how to act as apostles.' (Lenski) This makes the Corinthians realize the full shame of their disloyalty as nothing else would.

*V*21b: **Howbeit whereinsoever any is bold, (I speak fool–ishly,) I am bold also.**

Paul's lengthy preamble is over. Although the task is dis-agreeable, the moment has come when for the sake of the Corinthians he must cast modesty aside and launch into his 'foolish' boasting. This he does in the full confidence that he is well able to match any claim put forward by his rivals. For 'the grounds on which they shew their audacity are as much mine as theirs.' (Massie)

*V*22: **Are they Hebrews? so am I. Are they Israelites? so am I. Are they the seed of Abraham? so am I.**

That Paul should place this proud claim in the forefront of his apology would seem to indicate that his antagonists were Palestinian Jews who boasted of the purity of their descent in order to confine the Corinthians within the straitjacket of their Judaistic 'gospel.' But he insists that his own pedigree is in no sense inferior to theirs; he has inherited exactly the same privi-leges, though of course he attached a very different value to them. [cf. *Rom* 4:9-18] The three questions form a climax, — ' "Hebrews" referring to the *language* and *nationality;* "Israel-ites," to the *theocracy* and *descent from Israel*, the "prince who prevailed with God" [*Rom* 9:4]; "the seed of Abraham," to the *claim to a share in the promised* [*Gal* 3:29] Messiah [*Rom* 9:7; 11:1]. Cf. Phil 3:5, "an Hebrew of the Hebrews;" not an Hellenist or Greek-speaking Jew, but a Hebrew in tongue, sprung from Hebrews [cf. *Acts* 22:3].' (Fausset)

V23: Are they ministers of Christ? (I speak as a fool) I am more; in labours more abundant, in stripes above measure, in prisons more frequent, in deaths oft.

Are they ministers of Christ? . . . I more; (RV) 'i.e. I am more a minister of Christ than they, not I am more than a minister of Christ. "The more a man suffers," says Bengel, "the more he ministers".' (Goudge) As a minister of Christ Paul is far beyond them, because they are not ministers of Christ *at all* (*vv* 13, 15); so here he does not say 'So am I.'

(I speak as one beside himself) (RV) Paul knows that 'to glory about so sacred a matter as the service of Christ is downright madness.' (Plummer)

in labours – excessively! in prisons – excessively! in stripes – beyond measure! in deaths – often! (Lenski) The reality of Paul's ministry is so completely beyond the empty claims of the Judaizers that no comparison between them is possible. 'The sense is that regarding these four points the false ministers have nothing whatever to exhibit.' (Lenski) [cf. *Gal* 6:17]

V24: Of the Jews five times received I forty stripes save one.

Paul's laconic account of the terrible sufferings he had endured up to the time of writing this Epistle conveys a vivid impression of his extraordinary labours and forms a valuable supplement to the very selective outline of his life in Acts. (Bernard) On no less than five occasions he was sentenced by the Jews to be beaten within an inch of his life. Forty strokes was the maximum punishment which could be inflicted short of the death penalty [*Deut* 25:3], and this was later reduced to thirty-nine for fear of a miscount. 'Notice that the Jews, even in cruelty and injustice to a servant of God, were scrupulously careful to obey in an insignificant detail the letter of the Law. Cf. *Matt* 23:23.' (Beet) [*Matt* 10:17]

*V*25: **Thrice was I beaten with rods, once was I stoned, thrice I suffered shipwreck, a night and a day I have been in the deep;**

Of the three occasions when Paul was beaten by the Roman authorities we only have a record of the one at Philippi. [*Acts* 16:22, 23, 37) As Plummer points out, the fact that Paul 'was thrice treated in this way is evidence that being a Roman citizen was an imperfect protection when magistrates were disposed to be brutal.' Although Luke gives an account of the stoning at Lystra [*Acts* 14:19], he does not mention these shipwrecks, which of course took place before that recorded in Acts 27, but Paul made many voyages – Dr. P. E. Hughes calculates at least eighteen – and sailing was a risky business in those days.

a night and a day I have been adrift at sea; (RSV) This means that Paul was in (not under) the sea, probably clinging to some fragment of the wreck, in imminent peril of his life for twenty-four hours before being rescued. The tense may indicate that a recent experience is here vividly recalled.

*V*26: **In journeyings often, in perils of rivers, in perils of robbers, in perils from my countrymen, in perils from the Gentiles, in perils in the city, in perils in the wilderness, in perils in the sea, in perils among false brethren;** (RV)

A graphic description of the many hazards Paul continually faced in the prosecution of his apostolic commission, of which the last would be the most distressing. The pseudo-apostles also braved the dangers of first-century travel to reach Corinth with their false gospel, but none of *their* perils were like Paul's. 'Paul's were perils that were met with on *apostolic* journeys, theirs were perils such as the Pharisees encountered when they compassed sea and land to make one proselyte; "and when he is made, ye make him two-fold more the child of hell than yourselves," Matt 23:15.' (Lenski) How like the cultists today!

*V*27: **In weariness and painfulness, in watchings often, in hunger and thirst, in fastings often, in cold and nakedness.**

Through labour and hardship, through many a sleepless night, through hunger and thirst, starving many a time, cold and ill-clad. (Moffatt)

In addition to these perils, the physical privations Paul endured would have served to quench the ardour of a less indomitable spirit than his. The 'fastings' referred to here were not religious but quite involuntary. Moffatt gives the correct sense of the verse. 'When we remember that he who endured all this was a man constantly suffering from infirm health [2 *Cor* 4:7–12; 12:7–10; *Gal* 4:13, 14], such heroic self-devotion seems almost superhuman' (*Conybeare and Howson*).' (cited by Fausset)

*V*28: **Beside those things that are without, that which cometh upon me daily, the care of all the churches.**

besides the things that I do not mention, there is that which presses upon me daily, my anxiety for all the Churches. (Plummer) Paul could say much more along the same lines, but he wants the troublesome church in Corinth to understand that all these trials are as nothing compared with the daily pressure of his anxiety for all the churches. He regards this as his real burden; his other troubles are only the incidental extras he receives by way of a bonus! (Lenski) His evaluation is intended to startle the Corinthians, especially when it is contrasted with the callous indifference of the mercenary-minded hirelings they had been so ready to welcome as their true shepherds.

*V*29: **Who is weak, and I am not weak? who is offended, and I burn not?**

Paul's deep concern for the churches leads him to sympathize with the weak and to wax indignant against their seducers.

Who is weak, and I am not weak? He feels their weakness as though it were his own. Christian love is gentle and bears patiently with the weak, but carnal pride ruthlessly takes advantage of their weakness to impose its own will on them. Thus the weak Corinthians had succumbed to the boastful strength of the Judaizers!

If anyone is made to stumble, does my heart not blaze with indignation? (NEB) 'It was not to Paul a matter of indifference when any of the brethren, by the force of evil example, or by the seductions of false teachers, were led to depart from the truth or to act inconsistently with their profession. Such events filled him not only with grief at the fall of the weak, but with indignation at the authors of their fall.' (Hodge)

*V*30: **If I must needs glory, I will glory of the things which concern mine infirmities.**

This verse looks both ways. It sums up what has gone before (*vv* 23-28), and is the preface to what follows [12:5-10]. Paul had promised to join his adversaries in the foolishness of boasting, but his boasting has been of a very different character from theirs. For he does not boast of his achievements, but always of the things that concern his weakness. 'He set out to boast; see how he has done it! he has brought forward the very things a boastful person would have said nothing about. There is a boast for you! The Corinthians, carried away by the boasting of those other people, are now to look at this boast too, and see what they think of it.' (Menzies)

V31: **The God and Father of our Lord Jesus Christ, which is blessed for evermore, knoweth that I lie not.**

This solemn assurance vouches for the veracity of all that he has said and all that he has yet to say concerning his weakness, and was doubtless intended to counter the calumnies which were circulated about the reliability of his word. [1:17] As befits the servant of Him who cannot lie, Paul speaks only what 'the God and Father of the Lord Jesus' (RV) *knows* to be the truth. [cf. *Rom* 9:5 and see comment on 1:3]

V32: **In Damascus the governor under Aretas the king kept the city of the Damascenes with a garrison, desirous to apprehend me:**

V33: **And through a window in a basket was I let down by the wall, and escaped his hands.**

Many have wondered why Paul should have decided to mention his escape from Damascus at this particular point. The most reasonable explanation would seem to be that this experience marked the beginning of his 'weakness'. The name of Damascus was indelibly engraved upon the tablet of his memory because it was 'there that the persecutor became the persecuted.' (Waite) What a contrast there was between his arrogant approach to the city, and his humiliating exit from it! [cf. *Acts*

[147]

9:1-2; 23-25] Moreover, as Dr Hughes clearly shows, this account of Paul's inglorious escape is also in pointed contrast to the experience which he is about to describe. [12:2ff] 'The man who experienced the ineffable "ascent" even to the third heaven was the same man who had experienced the undistinguished "descent" from a window in the Damascus wall.'

Damascus was not part of the Nabataean kingdom which bordered it, but the governor (or ethnarch) of King Aretas had jurisdiction over the large Arabian colony in the city. In seeking to silence a notorious troublemaker, the Jews successfully enlisted the help of the governor who made arrangements for his clandestine arrest. 'The ethnarch had no authority to arrest Saul openly, as he would have had if Damascus had at this time been part of Aretas's realm.' (F. F. Bruce, *Commentary on the Book of the Acts*, p 204)

CHAPTER TWELVE

*V*1: **It is not expedient for me doubtless to glory. I will come to visions and revelations of the Lord.**

I am obliged to boast. (NEB) Paul introduces his final boast with a fresh apology. Such boasting is not delightful, but it is necessary. It is with the greatest reluctance that he brings forward an experience about which he has kept silent for four-teen years, and the only reason he does so now is in order to relate its sequel. (*vv* 7-10) Hence his purpose is again to reduce his boast to a 'boasting in weakness.' (Massie)

It does no good; (NEB) i.e. it is not useful or helpful. 'He means that he expects to confer no spiritual profit upon the Corinthians by telling them about this phenomenal experience of his.' (Lenski)

but I shall go on to tell of visions and revelations granted by the Lord. (NEB) The construction indicates the Lord as the source of the visions and revelations. 'It is not impossible, however, that a note of objectivity is intended as well, that is, that during the course of this experience Paul saw the risen and ascended Lord.' (P. E. Hughes) [cf. *Acts* 7:55] The visions Paul received had a revelatory function, but not every revelation that was made to him was visually mediated.[1]

[1]*It is important for Christians today to grasp the fact that the gospel would be incomplete if extra-Biblical revelations were necessary to supplement its teach-*

*V*2: **I knew a man in Christ above fourteen years ago, (whether in the body, I cannot tell; or whether out of the body, I cannot tell: God knoweth;) such an one caught up to the third heaven.**

I know a man in Christ, fourteen years ago (RV) 'Another person might shout: '*I, I*, have been in Paradise!' and exalt himself above all his fellow men. Another man might tell about it on every possible occasion. Paul kept it a secret for fourteen years; it is now forced from him only by utter necessity. Even under this compulsion he is able to tell about it only as though it had happened to another person.' (Lenski)

(whether in the body, I know not; or whether out of the body, I know not; God knoweth) (RV) 'Ignorance of the mode does not take away the certain knowledge of the thing.' (Bengel) Since Paul confessed his ignorance as to whether he was in or out of the body at the time, speculation on the matter is quite pointless, for we can hardly expect to establish what he

---

ing. Revelation is the interpretation of a redemption which is partly objective and partly subjective. Revelation keeps pace with the *objective acts* of redemption, the incarnation, the atonement, and the resurrection of Christ, but it does not accompany the *subjective application* of that redemption to the individual in regeneration, conversion, justification, and sanctification. This explains why redemption extends further than revelation. To insist upon revelation 'accompanying subjective-individual redemption would imply that it dealt with questions of private, personal concern, instead of with the common concerns of the world of redemption collectively.' (condensed and quoted from *Biblical Theology* by Geerhardus Vos, p. 14) This means that inspiration, in the full apostolic meaning of the word, ceased when the canon of Scripture was brought to completion. Without such *apostolic* inspiration there can be no *infallible* revelation. The only revelation from God which Christians still await is the Revelation of Jesus Christ at His Second Coming. And that will be objective enough to satisfy everyone that it has really taken place!

himself was unable to determine. What satisfied him, should satisfy us too: ' *God* knoweth.'

such an one caught up 'The same word describes how surviving Christians will be "caught up" to meet the descending Lord [1 *Thess* 4:17].' (Massie)

even to the third heaven. (RV) As Calvin sensibly remarks, Paul is not here drawing fine philosophical distinctions between the different heavens, but uses three as a perfect number to indicate what is highest and most complete. Thus 'not content with using the simple word heaven, Paul adds that he had reached its utmost height and innermost chambers.'

*V*3: **And I know such a man (whether in the body, or apart from the body, I know not; God knoweth),**

*V*4: **How that he was caught up into Paradise, and heard unspeakable words, which it is not lawful for a man to utter.** (RV) This solemn repetition prepares the way for some additional information about the same experience.

Paradise The first Paradise in Eden was 'lost' through sin, but through the triumph of grace that lost glory is 'regained' in the Paradise of heaven. [cf. *Luke* 23:34; *Rev* 2:7]

and heard unutterable utterances (Lenski) Paul heard the incommunicable, but he preached an intelligible message of salvation. 'Paul was not a "gnostic," but a witness; salvation, according to his teaching, came not through a mystic vision, but through the hearing of faith.' (J. G. Machen, *The Origin of Paul's Religion*, p 265)

which it is not lawful for a man to utter. 'If anyone retorts that in that case what Paul heard was superfluous and useless, for what good was there in hearing something that had to be held back in perpetual silence, my answer is that this thing happened for Paul's own sake, for a man who had awaiting him troubles hard enough to break a thousand hearts needed to be strengthened in a special way to keep him from giving way and to help him to persevere undaunted.' (Calvin)

V5: **Of such an one will I glory: yet of myself I will not glory, but in mine infirmities.**

'On behalf of one, who in all this was entirely passive and recipient, without exertion or merit of his own, he will boast, but not on behalf of his personal self, his own will, work and service, except with regard to his infirmities. He has already in mind the infirmity of *v* 7; the correlative of his visions and revelations.' (Waite)

V6: **For though I would desire to glory, I shall not be a fool; for I will say the truth: but now I forbear, lest any man should think of me above that which he seeth me to be, or that he heareth of me.**

If I should choose to boast, it would not be the boast of a fool, for I should be speaking the truth. (NEB) Paul cuts short his glorying even though he could say a great deal more, all of which would be nothing but the sober truth. 'Even in his great humility Paul takes care to leave no false impressions. He *was* something by the grace of God [*1 Cor* 15:10]. It would be falsehood to deny it even by implication, an implication which one might falsely deduce from the emphasis which Paul puts on his weakness as being his only boast.' (Lenski)

But I refrain, because I should not like anyone to form an estimate of me which goes beyond the evidence of

his own eyes and ears. (NEB) The apostle 'never makes mystical experience a ground of claiming apostolic authority. To his opponents such experiences would have been remarkable accomplishments, giving to their status and teaching an added authority and impressive kudos. Paul places no such value on ecstasy, nor does he imply that he was nearer to God then – when caught up into Paradise – than at other times under normal conditions. This is an important observation, which should set us on our guard against all forms of "mysticism" and exceptional experiences which are made the basis for some claim in a matter of Christian doctrine or practice.' (R. P. Martin)

*V*7: **And lest I should be exalted above measure through the abundance of the revelations, there was given to me a thorn in the flesh, the messenger of Satan to buffet me, lest I should be exalted above measure.**

And lest I should be exalted above measure through the abundance of the revelations, 'How dangerous must self-exaltation be, when even the apostle required so much restraint!' (Fausset)

there was given to me The gift was entirely unsolicited by Paul, but with the gift he was also given the grace to receive it as a favour!

a thorn in the flesh, Of this we know no more than Paul tells us here. That it was a recurring painful physical affliction is certain, but an exact diagnosis of the condition is impossible. Our ignorance remains even if Galatians 4:13, 14 may be legitimately linked with this verse. The most plausible guesses all fall short of final certainty. If it had been spiritually profitable for us to know the nature of this malady God would have told us. As it is, Paul's thorn in the flesh becomes 'by its very lack of definition, a type of every Christian's "thorn in the flesh", not with regard to externals, but by its spiritual significance.' (P. E. Hughes)

the messenger of Satan to buffet me, The case of Job furnishes a helpful parallel [*Job* 2:7], for it shows that it was within God's wise and holy purpose to prove the fidelity of His servant by sending Satan to do the evil work in which he takes a fiendish delight. [cf. *Luke* 13:16] Satan could not touch a hair of Job's head without leave, for absolutely nothing lies outside the scope of God's sovereignty. All God's creatures are subject to His ruling and over-ruling; and even the work of Satan is overruled so that it assists in bringing to pass the Divine purpose, though Satan on his part uses his utmost powers to thwart that purpose.

lest I should be exalted above measure. The Divine purpose in this affliction is repeated for emphasis. Satan's malice is always frustrated by God and made to minister a blessing *to His people*. The 'all things' of Romans 8:28 admits of no exceptions.

*V*8: **For this thing I besought the Lord thrice, that it might depart from me.**

On three occasions Paul made it a matter of earnest entreaty that the Lord Jesus would deliver him from the attacks of this messenger of Satan. In moments of physical suffering it is natural to seek relief from the One who is 'touched with the feeling of our infirmities' [*Heb* 4:15], 'and the Greek word for "besought" is one frequently used of the appeals of the sick in the Gospels.' (Goudge)

*V*9: **And he said unto me, My grace is sufficient for thee: for my strength is made perfect in weakness.** Most

gladly therefore will I rather glory in my infirmities, that the power of Christ may rest upon me.

And he hath said to me, (Bernard) 'The perfect tense denotes that what the Lord said was a *standing* answer valid for the Apostle's whole life.' (Waite)

My grace is sufficient for thee: for my power is made perfect in weakness. (RV) Paul reaches the climax of the entire Epistle in this revelation of the secret of his power, a secret whose meaning was far beyond the understanding of his boastful rivals. For the self-sufficient must ever remain strangers to the power of that grace which is manifested only in conscious weakness. 'The power of Christ manifests to the full its irresistible energy and attains its highest results by performing works of power with powerless instruments.' (Beet)

Most gladly therefore will I rather glory in my weaknesses, (RV) This unexpected answer resulted in a complete reversal of Paul's attitude towards his thorn in the flesh, so that he was now prepared to welcome the weaknesses which made his dependence upon the power of Christ so complete. Dr Hughes is careful to distinguish between Paul's weaknesses which were *given* him (*v* 7), and 'a joyless theology of insecurity' that encouraged men to try to accumulate merit before God through sufferings which were self-inflicted.

that the power of Christ may rest upon me. *lit.* 'may pitch its tent upon me' i.e. 'dwell in me as in a tent, as the shechinah dwelt of old in the tabernacle. To be made thus the dwelling-place of the power of Christ, where he reveals his glory, was a rational ground of rejoicing in those infirmities which were the condition of his presence and the occasion for the manifestation of his power.' (Hodge)

*V*10: **Therefore I take pleasure in infirmities, in reproaches, in necessities, in persecutions, in distresses for Christ's sake: for when I am weak, then am I strong.**

Wherefore I am well content in weaknesses, in insults, in necessities, in persecutions, and distresses, for Christ's sake; for whenever I am weak, then am I strong. (Bernard) As Dr. Tasker makes clear, the all-important words are 'for Christ's sake.' [*Matt* 5:11] 'Only a morbid fanatic can take pleasure in the sufferings he inflicts upon himself; only an insensitive fool can take pleasure in the sufferings that are the consequences of his folly; and only a convinced Christian can take pleasure in sufferings endured *for Christ's sake*, for he alone has been initiated into the divine secret, that it is only when he is *weak*, having thrown himself unreservedly in penitence and humility upon the never-failing mercies of God, that he is *strong*, with a strength not his own, but belonging to the "Lord of all power and might." '

*V*11: **I am become a fool in glorying; ye have compelled me: for I ought to have been commended of you: for in nothing am I behind the very chiefest apostles, though I be nothing.**

I am become foolish: ye compelled me; for I ought to have been commended of you: (RV) Paul admits that he has become foolish, but this foolishness was forced upon him by the disloyalty of the Corinthians. For if instead of receiving the slanders of his detractors, they had rushed to his defence, he would not have been compelled to descend to the folly of boasting in order to rescue them from the toils of false doctrine.

for in nothing did I fall short of the superlative apostles, nothing though I am. (Waite) ' "Nonentity" though I am, you have had ample proof that I did not fall short of these precious "apostles" of yours!' The charge hurled at Paul is a boomerang, for he has boasted of nothing but his own 'nothingness.' Yet this nothingness has been used as the vehicle of Divine power in Corinth, whereas the self-inflated pretensions of these superlative apostles have been productive of nothing more than the works of the flesh. 'The difference between this statement and that of 11:5, is that there he asserted a general and standing non-inferiority, whereas he here asserts a non-inferiority proved in his actual ministry among them. (aorist) Hence the clause is a transition-link to the appeal to facts (12ff.) with which they were acquainted.' (Waite)

*V*12: **Truly the signs of an apostle were wrought among you in all patience, in signs, and wonders, and mighty deeds.**

the signs that mark a true apostle were performed among you (but you paid no attention) (Arndt-Gingrich) The miraculous element in Paul's ministry should have convinced the Corinthians of the reality of his apostleship. For apostolic signs were the visible authentication of an apostolic commission. 'As the *signs* have not been transmitted to us, neither has the apostleship. The apostles have no literal successors [cf. *Acts* 1:21, 22].' (Fausset) It is obvious that such an appeal would have been ludicrous if the Corinthians had never witnessed such signs. By his use of the passive tense, Paul shows that he was but the instrument through whom the power of God was manifested in their midst.

in all patience, Not a sign, 'but the element IN which the signs were wrought.' (Fausset)

by signs and wonders and mighty works. (RV) 'He calls them *signs* because they are not merely meaningless spectacles

[157]

but are designed to instruct men. He calls them *wonders* because by their novelty they should rouse and astonish, and he calls them powers or *mighty works* because they are more evidently examples of divine power than those which we discover in the ordinary course of nature.' (Calvin) [cf. *Acts* 2:22; 2 *Thess* 2:9; *Heb* 2:4]

*V*13: **For what is it wherein ye were inferior to other churches, except it be that I myself was not burdensome to you? forgive me this wrong.**

Thus the ministry the Corinthians received from Paul was in no respect inferior to that which the rest of the churches received, unless it was in regard to his refusal to accept maintenance from them. With cutting irony he asks their forgiveness for this wrong! 'In my nothingness I did not ask even a penny of support. Pardon me for the great loss which you thus suffered!' (Lenski)

*V*14: **Behold, the third time I am ready to come to you; and I will not be burdensome to you: for I seek not yours, but you: for the children ought not to lay up for the parents, but the parents for the children.**

Paul is now ready to pay them his third visit and he will not be a burden to them this time any more than he was on his two previous visits, the first of which took place when he founded the church, and the second towards the end of his stay in Ephesus. He followed this short sorrowful visit with the 'lost' letter referred to in 1 *Cor* 5:9. [cf. 2:1 and see Introduction]

for I seek not yours, but you: Paul has a far greater goal in view than a share of their wealth; he seeks their full salvation through the grace of God in Christ Jesus. He cares not for their

goods so long as he can gain their souls. His concern is not for
the wool, but for the sheep. (Lenski) [cf. 1 *Pet* 5:2]

children . . . parents As their spiritual father [1 *Cor* 4:14;15],
Paul does not seek earthly treasure *from* them, but rather seeks
to lay up heavenly treasure *for* them.

*V*15: **And I will very gladly spend and be spent for you;
though the more abundantly I love you, the less I be
loved.**

**But *I*, I will most gladly spend, and be utterly spent for
the good of your souls.** (Plummer) 'This is proof of an
affection that is more than fatherly, since he was ready to
expend in their service not only his work and whatever substance he might possess, but his life as well.' (Calvin)

If I love you more abundantly, am I loved the less?
(RV) i.e. 'Are you going to let your love diminish as fast as
my love increases? That would be a strange kind of return to
make, a strange instance of inverse proportion!' (Plummer)

*V*16: **But be it so, I did not burden you: nevertheless,
being crafty, I caught you with guile.**

That Paul himself had never been a burden on the Corinthians'
resources could not be disputed by anyone, but his detractors
had not been above hinting that he had profited from them
in other ways. The insinuation was that 'with my natural craft,
I caught you by my ostentatious disinterestedness, and then
all the more successfully plundered you through my agents.'
(Massie)

*V*17: **Did I make a gain of you by any of them whom I
sent unto you?**

With respect to any one of those whom I have sent to you, did I outwit you through him for gain? (P. E. Hughes) Paul throws down the challenge in the confidence that the transparent honesty of his assistants speaks for itself. They have given the Corinthians no occasion to doubt their integrity at any time.

*V*18: **I desired Titus, and with him I sent a brother. Did Titus make a gain of you? walked we not in the same spirit? walked we not in the same steps?**

I exhorted Titus, and I sent the brother with him. (RV) 'The mission of Titus to Corinth here referred to, is not that mentioned in ch 8, which was not yet accomplished, but that mentioned in ch 7, designed to ascertain the effect produced by Paul's previous letter.' (Hodge)

surely Titus took no advantage of you? walked we not by the same spirit and in the same steps? (Bernard) Paul can fairly appeal to the success of Titus in winning the trust of the Corinthians, for the character and conduct of the messenger was a faithful reflection of the apostle upon whose instructions he had acted.

*V*19: **Again, think ye that we excuse ourselves unto you? we speak before God in Christ: but we do all things, dearly beloved, for your edifying.**

Have you been thinking all along that I have been de-fending myself *before you*? (J. H. Moulton cited by P. E. Hughes) Paul's self-vindication is complete but he does not want the Corinthians to run away with the idea that he stands before their tribunal in the hope of securing a favourable verdict.

In the sight of God speak we in Christ. (RV) It is not to *men* that Paul holds himself accountable [1 *Cor* 4:3], for it is in the sight of God and in union with Christ that he so speaks [cf. 2:17].

But every word, beloved, we speak for your edification. (Plummer) 'So far as his authority in Corinth was undermined, so far were they tottering and it was necessary to reconsolidate *his* position in order that *theirs* might be restored and secured.' (Waite)

*V*20: **For I fear, lest, when I come, I shall not find you such as I would, and that I shall be found unto you such as ye would not: lest there be debates, envyings, wraths, strifes, backbitings, whisperings, swellings, tumults:**

For I fear that perhaps I may come and find you not what I wish, and that you may find me not what you wish; (RSV) Although Paul has spoken so sternly, it has been with a view to their edification, for he fears that when he comes he may find them in a different state than *he* would wish, i.e. still wallowing in the same sins which called forth his 'severe' letter (1 Corinthians). In that case, they would find him to be other than *they* would wish, i.e. severe in punishing their misconduct. He gently gives expression to his fear in the hope that they will take the opportunity to remove all occasion for such severity before he arrives in Corinth.

lest by any means there should be strife, jealousy, (RV) Contention and envying. (Fausset) **wraths, factions,** (RV) Fits of temper and party-intrigues. (Tasker) **backbitings, whisperings,** Open slander and secret gossip. **swellings, tumults:** Swellings of pride and grave disorders. (P. E. Hughes)

*V*21: **And lest, when I come again, my God will humble me among you, and that I shall bewail many which**

**have sinned already, and have not repented of the un–
cleanness and fornication and lasciviousness which they
have committed.**

Lest, when I come, my God should *again* **humble me
before you,** (Plummer) Having once visited them in sorrow
[2:1], Paul fears a further humiliation may be in store for him
on his return to Corinth. 'Nothing brings a Christian teacher
into the dust so much as the defection of those whom he has
looked on as fruits of his labour and as his crown of rejoicing.'
(Beet)

**and I may have to mourn over many of those who sinned
before and have not repented of the impurity, immor–
ality, and licentiousness which they have practised.**
(RSV) Paul sorrowfully refers to those Corinthians who
having relapsed into their old pagan ways remained impenitent
under his reproofs. His coming will discover whether he
must mourn over them as those who are spiritually dead.

CHAPTER THIRTEEN

*V*1: **This is the third time I am coming to you. In the mouth of two or three witnesses shall every word be established.**

Paul abruptly announces the imminence of his *third* visit. That he *is* coming is certain, but the manner of his visit will depend upon the Corinthians' attitude towards him. He wishes no one to be in the slightest doubt of his determination to deal with the recalcitrant in accordance with the principles of justice laid down by Moses and endorsed by Christ. [*Deut* 19:15; *Matt* 18:16] 'Paul's word is intended as a warning. He has just mentioned repentance [12:21]. He hopes that there will be no unrepentant sinners with whom he must deal when he arrives. They will get a fair trial, indeed, but a trial they will get.' (Lenski)

*V*2: **I told you before, and foretell you, as if I were present, the second time; and being absent now I write to them which heretofore have sinned, and to all other, that, if I come again, I will not spare:**

As Bengel notes, there is in the text, which excludes 'I write' as an inferior reading, 'an uninterrupted chiasmus throughout the three members of the sentence,' which Dr Hughes sets out as follows:

I have said beforehand and I do say beforehand
↓ ↓
when I was present the and now being absent
second time
↓ ↓
to them that have sinned and to all the rest
heretofore

Paul has already warned those who were leading sinful lives at the time of his second visit that if he came again he would not spare them, and now he reiterates the warning to all others whom he may find in the same sinful state when he arrives in Corinth for the third time.

if I come again, The meaning is: 'when I come this time.' (NEB) It would be ridiculous to take the 'if' as expressing uncertainty over the much-advertised visit. 'All that is meant is that the punishment depends on the coming, whenever that takes place.' (Massie)

I will not spare; Paul hopes that it will not be necessary to provide the Corinthians with the proof that he means what he says (*vv* 7, 10), but those who disregard this final warning must realize that they leave their apostle with no alternative. (*v* 3)

*V*3: **Since ye seek a proof of Christ speaking in me, which to you-ward is not weak, but is mighty in you.**

I will not spare; seeing that ye seek a proof of Christ that speaketh in me; (RV) This is closely connected with the previous verse. Since the rebellious minority demand a proof that Christ speaks in Paul, they shall have what they want! It is possible that there is an implied contrast with his opponents' claim to be the true spokesmen of Christ. Thus Waite comments; 'The words "*in me*" are obviously emphatic, and show that the Christ who spoke *in him* is contrasted with the Christ which spoke in the Judaizers. In accordance with their entire system, they ascribed the weakness shown on his second visit to the Christ whom he preached and who, being not a legal, but a spiritual Christ, they said was powerless to enforce obedience to law. Thus they challenged his Christ to a proof of his power. The libertines by their defiance did the same thing, for if they did not take up the taunt of the Judaizers, they clearly counted upon the same weakness for escaping punishment altogether [1 *Cor* 5:2, 6].'

who to you-ward is not weak, but is powerful in you: (RV) 'Of Christ's power *towards* and *among* the Corinthians, Paul has already given full proof, viz. [12:12] the miracles wrought in their midst and [3:2] the spiritual effects of the Gospel in their hearts. He will now add the more terrible proof of special punishment.' (Beet)

*V*4: **For though he was crucified through weakness, yet he liveth by the power of God. For we also are weak in him, but we shall live with him by the power of God toward you.**

For he was crucified through weakness, yet he liveth through the power of God. (RV) As it was in virtue of His self-assumed weakness that Christ was once crucified, so it is in virtue of the power of God that He now lives forever as the triumphant Son of Man. It would be folly to presume on a temporary weakness, and to forget the present reality of Christ's power to punish as well as to save. For 'the cross does *not* exhaust Christ's relation to sin; He passed from the cross to the throne, and when He comes again it is as Judge.' (Denney)

For we also are weak in him, but we shall live with him through the power of God toward you. (RV) If Paul has experienced in full measure what it means to be weak in Christ, he is no stranger to that Divine power which is made perfect in weakness. Thus though his 'painful' visit was marked by a weakness which the Corinthians despised, when he comes again he will act towards them with a power which will command their respect! The believer's future inheritance is not in view here.

*V*5: **Examine yourselves, whether ye be in the faith; prove your own selves. Know ye not your own selves, how that Jesus Christ is in you, except ye be reprobates?**

Try your own selves, whether ye be in the faith; prove your own selves. (RV) Instead of putting Paul's apostleship to the proof (*v* 3), the Corinthians should be testing the genuineness of their own faith in Christ! If, as Paul expects, most of them find that this self-examination confirms the reality of their attachment to Christ, then it must also show that he has exercised an authentic ministry among them. [3:2; 1 *Cor* 9:2]

Or know ye not as to your own selves, that Jesus Christ is in you? unless indeed ye be reprobate. (RV) In this passage 'reprobate' is not used in the theological sense of being judicially abandoned to everlasting perdition; it means 'failing to pass the test, unapproved, counterfeit,' (Souter) 'They ought to recognize Christ as a power in themselves – unless indeed they, being counterfeit Christians, cannot recognize Him because He is not there.' (Massie)

*V*6: **But I hope that ye shall know that we are not reprobate.** (RV) But should any among them prove to be such counterfeit Christians, Paul hopes to convince them that at least *he* is not a counterfeit apostle! For faithfulness to his commission will compel him to mete out condign punishment to the faithless in Corinth.

*V*7: **Now I pray to God that ye do no evil; not that we should appear approved, but that ye should do that which is honest, though we be as reprobates.**

Now we pray to God that ye do no evil; not that we may appear approved, but that ye may do that which is honourable, (RV Paul, however, prays that the Corinthians may do that which is noble and right, for he has no desire to demonstrate his apostolic authority by inflicting punishment. His first concern is not with his own reputation, but with the spiritual well-being of his converts.

though we be as reprobate. (RV) Hence if none deserved punishment he would not be disappointed, even though in failing to carry out a threatened judgment he might *seem like* a counterfeit apostle.

*V*8: **For we can do nothing against the truth but for the truth.**

For we have not any power against the truth, but for the truth. (Waite) 'Should those who had fallen away from the true Gospel [11:3] return, should those who had violated the obligations of love [12:20] and purity [12:21] repent, the cause of truth, doctrinal and practical, would be thus far re-established, and his power of chastising would be nullified, because in its very nature, capable of being applied only for and never against the truth.' (Waite)

*V*9: **For we are glad, when we are weak, and ye are strong: and this also we wish, even your perfection.**

For we rejoice, when we are weak, and ye are strong: (RV) 'When, in consequence of your strength in grace and

[167]

well-doing as a church we have no occasion to put forth our strength among you, but in all our own weakness look on, "joying and beholding your order and the steadfastness of your faith in Christ" [*Col* 2:5].' (Brown)

this we also pray for, even your perfecting. (RV) In fact this is the burden of Paul's prayer for them. That in a body which has been rent by factions there might be 'a resetting of what has been broken and dislocated, and hence a restoration of harmonious and efficient functioning.' (P. E. Hughes)

*V*10: **Therefore I write these things being absent, lest being present I should use sharpness, according to the power which the Lord hath given me to edification, and not to destruction.**

For this cause I write these things while absent, that I may not when present deal sharply, according to the authority which the Lord gave me for building up, and not for casting down. (RV) 'He would not write to them severely from a distance [10:10] except for the purpose of avoiding severity of action when present. With all his resolve to punish, with all the authority which the Lord gave him to punish, he will do anything rather than punish. This he expresses by repeating what he said in 10:8, that the true end for which his authority was given him was to build up and not to pull down. However necessary or beneficial chastisement may be, it is still "a pulling down," because it is, in the form here contemplated by him, plucking out stones, for a season at least, from the temple of the Lord. It is that evil which he prays they may not bring about (*v*:7).' (Waite)

*V*11: **Finally, brethren, farewell. Be perfect, be of good comfort, be of one mind, live in peace; and the God of love and peace shall be with you.**

In this final appeal Paul sums up his message to the Corinthians.

Mend your ways, heed my appeal, (RSV) Their many deficiencies must be amended, for the wholeness (or holiness) of the body to which they belong depends upon the harmonious working together of its many members. [cf *v*:9] But if this desirable end is to be attained in Corinth, they must so heed his appeal as to act upon it.

be of the same mind; live in peace: (RV) They must seek to be 'of the same mind in the Lord' [*Phil* 4:2], for they can only live in peace when they set their minds on the same thing. To have the mind of Christ is to banish that selfish individualism of thought which always results in strife.

and the God of love and peace shall be with you. 'We have here the familiar Christian paradox. God's presence produces love and peace, and we must have love and peace in order to have his presence. God gives what he commands. God gives, but we must cherish his gifts. His agency does not supersede ours, but mingles with it and becomes one with it in our consciousness. We work out our own salvation, while God works in us.' (Hodge) [*Phil* 2:12, 13] Thus the believer becomes actively engaged in doing the will of God through the enabling power of the same Spirit by whom he was first quickened.

*V*12: **Greet one another with an holy kiss.**

'The kiss was the expression of fellowship and affection. It was and is in the East the common mode of salutation among friends ... It is not a command of perpetual obligation, as the spirit of the command is that Christians should express their mutual love in the way sanctioned by the age and community in which they live.' (Hodge)

*V*I3: **All the saints salute you.**

'The saints who all salute the Corinthians are of course those with whom Paul is in touch when despatching the Epistle, i.e. the Christians of Macedonia, with any others from a distance who might be with him.' (Menzies)

*V*I4: **The grace of the Lord Jesus Christ, and the love of God, and the communion of the Holy Ghost, be with you all. Amen.**

'Remarkable it is that an Epistle written under a tempest of conflicting emotions, breathing in some places indignation, reproach, and sadness, at being driven to self-vindication against worthless detractors who should never have been listened to – that precisely this Epistle is the one that closes with the richest and most comprehensive of all the benedictions in the New Testament, the one which the Christian Church in every land and of every age has found, and will find as long as the world lasts, the most available for public use, as a close to its worship.' (Brown)

The grace of the Lord Jesus Christ, The Pauline gospel is summed up in the word which is his distinctive signature in every epistle. He who was once the implacable enemy of gospel grace is now its doughtiest defender. As the unworthy recipient of God's grace, he is inexorably opposed to the self-sufficient moralism by which it is subverted, always insistent that it comes to helpless sinners as the unmerited favour of God in Christ. It cannot be bought; it cannot be earned; it must be received as a free gift. Hence the order here is the order of Christian experience, for it is only through the grace of the Lord Jesus Christ that sinners come to know the love of God for them. The full title sets forth the majesty of the Mediator. 'Lord' points to His essential Deity, 'Jesus' underlines His genuine humanity so willingly assumed for our salvation, while 'Christ' tells us that He is the Messiah, the anointed fulfiller of the promised redemption.

and the love of God, Although God loved His people with an everlasting love, His holiness could not overlook the reality of their fearful fall into sin. In the resolution of this dilemma at the Cross, the Divine wisdom comes to its sublimest expression. It is there that all the attributes of God are seen to harmonize in the dread judgment that vindicated His justice even as it published His mercy. Thus the eternal love of God was the secret source of that matchless grace through which there is now manifested the marvel of the Father's adopting love.

and the communion of the Holy Spirit, (ARV) Apart from the Cross there can be no real understanding of God's love, while the only lasting fellowship between men is the fellowship of sinners redeemed by Christ's blood. (Tasker) It is the work of the Holy Spirit to bring about this fellowship by applying the benefits of that redemption to the hearts of God's people. It is therefore upon His gracious work that the individual and corporate spiritual life of believers entirely depends.

be with you all. Here is the measure of Paul's magnanimity; his love enbraces *all* the Corinthians, even those who have been the most disaffected towards him.

'The distinct personality and the divinity of the Son, the Father, and the Holy Spirit, to each of whom prayer is addressed, is here taken for granted. And therefore this passage is a clear recognition of the doctrine of the Trinity, which is the fundamental doctrine of Christianity. For a Christian is one who seeks and enjoys the grace of the Lord Jesus, the love of God, and the communion of the Holy Ghost.' (Hodge)

Soli Deo Gloria

BIBLIOGRAPHY

Arndt, W. F.-Gingrich, F. W. *A Greek-English Lexicon of the New Testament* [University of Chicago Press, 1957]

Beet, J. A. *II Corinthians* [H & S, 1882]

Bengel, J. A. *Gnomon of the New Testament* Vol. III [T & T Clark, 1857]

Bernard, J. H. *II Corinthians* (EGT) [H & S, 1903]

Boettner, Loraine *The Reformed Doctrine of Predestination* [P & R, 1965]

Brown, David. *II Corinthians* (Popular Commentary on the NT) [T & T Clark, 1882]

Bruce, F. F. *An Expanded Paraphrase of the Epistles of Paul* [Paternoster, 1965]

Bruce F. F. *The Acts of the Apostles* (NLCNT) [MMS, 1956]

Bruner, Frederick Dale. *A Theology of the Holy Spirit* [H & S, 1971]

Calvin, John. *II Corinthians – Philemon* [Oliver & Boyd, 1964]

Dabney, R. L. *Discussions: Evangelical and Theological* Vol. I [B of T, 1967]

Denney, James. *II Corinthians* (EB) [H & S, 1894]

Denney, James. *The Death of Christ* [Tyndale, 1964]

Dickson, David. *The Psalms* [B of T, 1959]

Douglas, J. D. (Editor) *The New Bible Dictionary*

Fairbairn, Patrick. *The Interpretation of Prophecy* [B of T, 1964]

Fausset, A. R. *II Corinthians* (JFB) [Collins, 1874]

Geldenhuys, Norval. *Supreme Authority* [MMS, 1953]

Goudge, H. L. *II Corinthians* (WC) [Methuen, 1927]

Hodge, A. A. *The Confession of Faith* [B of T, 1958]

Hodge, Charles. *II Corinthians* [B of T, 1959]

Hughes, Philip E. *II Corinthians* (NLCNT) [MMS, 1961]

Lenski, R. C. H. *The Interpretation of I & II Corinthians* [Augsburg, 1961]

Lightfoot, J. B. *Philippians* [Zondervan, 1968]

Lightfoot, J. B. *Notes on the Epistles of St. Paul* [Zondervan, 1957]

Machen, J. G. *The Origin of Paul's Religion* [Eerdmans, 1925]

Martin, R. P. *I Corinthians – Galatians* [SU, 1968]

Massie, J. *Corinthians* (Century Bible) [T. C. & E. C. Jack, 1902]

Meeter, John E. (Editor) *The Shorter Writings of B. B. Warfield* Vol. I [P & R, 1970]

Menzies, Allan. *II Corinthians* [Macmillan, 1912]

Murray, John. *Redemption-Accomplished and Applied* [B of T, 1961]

Poole, Matthew. *A Commentary on the Holy Bible*, Vol. III [B of T, 1963]

Pink, Arthur W. *Gleanings from Paul* [Moody, 1967]

Plummer, A. *II Corinthians* (ICC) [T & T Clark, 1915]

Ridderbos, Herman. *Paul and Jesus* [P & R, 1957]

Smeaton, George. *The Apostles' Doctrine of the Atonement* [Zondervan, 1957]

Souter, A. *A Pocket Lexicon to the Greek New Testament* [Oxford, 1956]

Tasker, R. V. G. *II Corinthians* [Tyndale, 1958]

Trapp, John. *Commentary on the New Testament* [SGBC, 1958]

Trench, R. C. *Synonyms of the New Testament* [James Clarke, 1961]

Vine, W. E. *Expository Dictionary of New Testament Words* [Oliphants, 1958]

Vos, Geerhardus. *Biblical Theology* [Eerdmans, 1948]

Vos, Geerhardus. *Pauline Eschatology* [Eerdmans, 1961]

Waite, J. *II Corinthians* (Speaker's Commentary) [John Murray, 1881]

Warfield, B. B. *The Plan of Salvation* [Eerdmans, 1955]